Henrietta Sees It Through

by the same author

AND THEN THERE WAS ONE

HENRIETTA'S WAR

HENRIETTA SEES IT THROUGH

MORE NEWS FROM THE HOME FRONT

1942–1945

JOYCE DENNYS

ANDRE DEUTSCH

The author and publisher
gratefully acknowledge permission granted
by the *Illustrated London News*
Archive and Picture Library to reproduce
material which originally appeared
in the *Sketch*

This collection first published by
André Deutsch Limited
105–106 Great Russell Street London WC1B 3LJ

British Library Cataloguing in Publication Data

Dennys, Joyce
  Henrietta sees it through: more news
  from the home front 1942–1945.
  I. Title
  828'.91408   PR6007.E57

ISBN 0–233–97970–0

      Printed in Great Britain by
Ebenezer Baylis & Son Ltd. Worcester

FOR MY GRANDDAUGHTERS
DEBORAH, PRUE AND JULIE

A NOTE FOR THE NEW READER

All you need to know in order to enjoy this book without having read its delightful predecessor* is that Henrietta is Joyce Dennys herself, Charles is her husband, Linnet their daughter and Perry their dog. All the other characters, including Robert, to whom the letters are addressed, are invented.

The setting is a small coastal town in Devon and you will soon realise that Lady B and Mrs Savernack are, in their different ways, sturdy upholders of a particularly English way of life and that Faith, the lively divorcée, is engaged in a long flirtation with the Conductor (an army reject sent to the mild South West for his health). The Visitors are people of some means who suddenly find that they prefer country life, and other characters need no explanation. In one of the many charming letters which had to be left out in compiling this little volume (the letters appeared first in the *Sketch* magazine—a weekly publication which became fortnightly as paper got scarcer) Colonel Simpkins is asked to come to a fund-raising fancy-dress party as Colonel Blimp and, to his surprise, is told there is no need to dress up. . .

We venture to predict that anyone who has not read the first volume will want to turn to it on reading this. The earlier instalment lacks the friendly presence of the Americans (quartered now in the South West in preparation for the invasion of Europe) but in its place possesses a special kind of innocence. The deep patriotic feeling which launched this unprepared and unprotected country on the long road to victory is still apparent in the present volume,

Henrietta's War News from the Home Front, 1939–1942 (Deutsch London 1985)

7

but so are the signs of fatigue and distress. Tempers are beginning to fray. There are moments of despair.

It is Joyce Dennys's great gift to have transformed the frustration and grief of those years into the most enchanting comedy. Perhaps a key to her unique quality as writer and illustrator lies in her determination to be not just the Doctor's Wife but herself as well.

M Y DEAR ROBERT
Is there anything more fascinating than cutting the edges of the lawn? I have an implement for doing this. I don't know its official name, but I call it the cutter which sounds more like a ship than anything else. I keep it sharpened and wrapped in oily paper, and guard it with my very life. The Linnet asked me once whether I loved my cutter more than her. I was deeply shocked by the question; but after considering the matter dispassionately for some hours, I came to the conclusion that, after Charles, Linnet, Bill, Perry and Lady B, my cutter came next, and a long way in front of Aunt Julia, Mrs Savernack and Cousin William. Twice a year I tenderly unwrap the cutter and slice bits off the edge of the lawn and all round the rose beds. I count these hours among the most vivid of my life. The bits that are sliced off look like delicious chocolate cake with green icing, and the gardener gathers them up greedily and hides them in the potting shed. He says they save Charles thirty shillings a year. I don't know what he uses them for. Bill says he eats them.

I was engaged upon this fascinating pursuit yesterday afternoon, when Lady B arrived and sat down on a garden seat in the sun to watch me.

'I can't think why you grumble about gardening,' she said after a few minutes.

'It isn't always bliss like this,' I said, pressing the cutter into the turf with a soft, squelching sound.

'You've left a little bulge there, Henrietta.'

'Here?'

'Further along. Yes, that's right. I suppose I couldn't do a little bit?'

'No.'

'I was afraid you'd say that,' said Lady B, so wistfully that my heart smote me.

'Oh, all right,' I said, grudgingly handing her the cutter. 'You can do to the corner.'

But Lady B waved it away. 'I don't really want to,' she said. 'You go on.'

Not want to use the cutter? I went and sat beside her and gazed earnestly into her face. 'You're not feeling ill, are you?' I said.

'No.' This in a very small voice.

'Darling Lady B, what is the matter?'

Lady B looked at me piteously. 'It's elastic,' she said.

'Elastic?'

'I suppose you realise there isn't going to be any soon?'

'I hadn't. But now you mention it, I suppose there isn't.'

'Nothing to keep our hats on with. Nothing to keep our stockings up with. Nothing to keep our—— I mean, how else *can* you keep a bust-bodice in place?'

'Nothing to keep our stockings up with'

I sat in stunned silence.

Lady B leaned towards me and said in a low voice: 'And then there's *stays*.'

'Is there?' I said dully.

'It's all very well for skinny people like you,' said Lady B—and I knew how upset she must be to call me skinny, for she is practically the only person here who is kind enough to describe me as slim. 'It doesn't matter whether *you* wear stays or not, but for me they are a necessity. Henrietta,' she said solemnly, laying her hand on my arm, 'for the last thirty years I have worn the same sort of stays. They are very expensive and very comfortable, and they have a wide piece of elastic down each side. I think I can say without undue conceit that they have proved successful, for my figure, though full, is not in any way ungainly. In fact, there are those who have described it as neat.'

'I never saw a neater.'

'But from now on I shall have to stay in bed!'

There was a tragic silence, and I picked up the cutter and did from top to bottom of the south side of the lawn, thinking hard all the time. It looked a bit crooked when I'd finished, so I did from bottom to top, but still thinking. Then I went back to the seat where Lady B was sitting gazing into an empty future, and took one of her clean hands in both my dirty ones.

'Listen,' I said, 'I don't think it's going to be as bad as all that. You must order some new stays at once. Perhaps we shall have won the war before they are worn out; but even if we haven't, they'll probably put us on Points for elastic, and you can have all mine and Charles's, except for his braces and sock-suspenders, and I really don't see why those shouldn't be knitted of wool.'

Lady B embraced me tenderly. 'I knew you'd cheer me up,' she said. Then we heard feet on the gravel and Mrs Savernack came round the corner.

'No wonder the Russians think we aren't working hard enough,' she said grimly, and I got guiltily to my feet.

'We were talking about my stays,' said Lady B, who was now quite cheerful again.

'Stays? Pah!' said Mrs Savernack. 'You'd be a great deal better if you didn't wear them.'

'And you'd be a——' I began, but Lady B gently but very firmly pressed my foot and shook her head at me.

Mrs Savernack picked up my cutter and ran an appreciative thumb around its edge. 'Nice implement,' she said. 'I'll finish this job for you.'

'Oh, please don't bother, Mrs Savernack!' I cried.

But Mrs Savernack, ignoring me, was squinting along the edge of the lawn which I had just done. 'My dear Henrietta,' she said, 'this is frightfully crooked,' and she started on a new line of her own while I pranced beside her uttering little cries of frustration and distress. Lady B remarked that our lawn was looking much smaller than it used to.

'There you are,' said Mrs Savernack, and she handed me back the cutter, which I grasped feverishly in my arms like a mother receiving back her child from the hands of strangers.

She started on a new line of her own

Then she stood on the rake, which flew up and hit the back of her head—but Lady B's eye was upon me and I never even smiled.

Always your affectionate Childhood's Friend,

HENRIETTA

M Y Dear Robert
Whenever we meet Visitors they say to us, 'And how does your British Restaurant work down here?'

'There isn't one,' we reply, hanging our heads.

'What! No British Restaurant?' they cry, looking at us askance as though we were the West Country Quislings. 'What you all need is a stick of bombs to wake you up.'

Those people here whose homes have actually been destroyed by bombs, or who have suffered loss and anxiety on account of the war, take these remarks very much to heart, and at last feeling ran so high that it was decided to hold a public meeting and discuss the subject thoroughly.

We always hold our meetings here at half-past seven, which is the hour when Charles staggers into his home with a white face, demanding whisky and a hot meal, and likes to find his wife sitting by the fire mending his pyjamas. Bill and the Linnet say that to complete the picture I ought to be rocking a cradle with my foot, but when they repeated this to Charles he shuddered and said 'God forbid!'

When I arrived at the meeting at seven thirty-five, having left an apologetic note for Charles propped against the whisky decanter, the hall was nearly full. Lady B was there, representing the Women's Institute, Mrs Savernack representing the Miniature Rifle Club, Mrs Whinebite the Mothers' Union, Admiral Marsdon the Urban District Council, Colonel Simpkins the Specials, Faith the A.R.P., and the Conductor the Women's Choir. I could tell a lot of other people were representing other things, too, by the solemn expression on their faces. The W.V.S., representing the W.V.S., made a nice green patch in the middle of the hall. My neighbour whispered to me that their uniform had been designed by a famous couturier but, be that as it may, it certainly is nice, and proves once for all that uniform can be becoming as well as serviceable.

13

At twenty to eight the Admiral opened proceedings by saying that the meeting had been called with a view to discussing the possibility of starting a British Restaurant. Then he sat down and there was a long and embarrassing silence. At the end of five minutes little Mrs Simpkins, unable to bear it any longer, pretended her nose was bleeding and left the hall.

Then Lady B stood up, amid a burst of hysterical cheering, and said she thought a British Restaurant would be a good idea, whereupon Mrs Savernack jumped to her feet and said Lady B was one of her oldest friends and she was sorry to contradict her in public, but that she, Mrs Savernack, was quite sure it would *not* be a good idea, especially if it were true that the rifle range was going to be taken over as a kitchen.

The Admiral said the point was, who would run it? All eyes were turned on the W.V.S. Eyes always are turned on the W.V.S. when somebody asks this sort of question. I sometimes wonder if they get tired of it.

The Head W.V.S. rose to say that they had a scheme worked out all ready to be put into use.

Faith said Lord Woolton had told us that it was a way in which we might augment our rations.

I said I would be very glad to augment our rations when the Linnet came home for her day off.

Mrs Whinebite turned on me, and with blazing eyes asked if I realised that it would mean the break-up of Home Life, and I said 'Why?'

Everybody became very angry. It had been a long and trying winter, and all the pent-up irritations of months were suddenly let loose. Shouts were heard, fists were shaken, and people who up till then hadn't cared a hoot whether we had a British Restaurant or not found themselves fighting passionately on one side or the other.

'Ladies and gentlemen—please!' said the Admiral.

'It's nothing but a ramp to deprive the poor trades-man of his due.'

'The Wrong People would use it.'

'I'm sure *I* don't want a British Restaurant.'

'If you had no maids and three evacuees instead of a P.G. at four guineas a week, you might.'

'Women ought to learn to shoot instead of cooking.'

'I know the Sanctity of the Home means nothing to Bohemians like you, Mrs Brown,' said Mrs Whinebite, who seemed to hold me responsible for the whole thing.

'Henrietta is *not* a Bohemian!'

'Yes I am!'

'Ladies and gentlemen, *please!*'

A little man who had been standing by the platform, holding up his hand for at least five minutes, suddenly commanded silence. 'I think it is only fair to inform the meeting,' he said, 'that the Chamber of Commerce has voted unanimously against a British Restaurant.'

After that we all went home quietly, because, of course, it's not the slightest good trying to run a restaurant without the co-operation of the tradesmen.

'*The Sanctity of the Home means nothing to Bohemians like you*'

15

Next morning in the Street I saw a vaguely familiar face smiling at me.

'Hullo, Mrs Brown!'

'How nice to see you down here again,' I said. This is what I always say to Visitors while I am trying to remember who they are.

'You remember my arm?'

'Of course.'

'My doctor was absolutely astonished at the result. He said he couldn't have done it better himself. You might tell Doctor Brown.'

'I will!'

'Well, how are you getting on? Of course, one simply wouldn't know there was a war on down here.'

'Wouldn't one?'

'How is your British Restaurant working?'

'Look!' I said. 'There's Lady B. You remember Lady B, don't you?'

'Why, yes!' cried the Visitor, and dived across the road, while I slipped into the chemist's to have a little chat about soap.

Always your affectionate Childhood's Friend,

HENRIETTA

March 11, 1942

MY DEAR ROBERT

Faith has resigned from the A.R.P. and joined the W.A.A.F.s. She said she simply couldn't bear reading about Germany's stupendous preparations for their spring offensive and go on living more or less comfortably at home any longer. We all think this is a tremendous gesture on her part, because, of course, she isn't as young as she was, and has always lived a rather luxurious sort of life. The Conductor, naturally, is distraught, and is moving heaven and earth to get into the Air Force, which he hasn't the faintest chance of doing. Faith was rather worried about her little W.A.A.F. hat at first. She said it was years since she had worn a hat really *on* her head, but she has got used to it now, and the result is a fair treat.

Lady B and I are wildly jealous. We, too, have guilty feelings about living in our homes, and last week Lady B went and offered herself to the A.T.S. 'I am seventy-five,' she said, 'and I know you are thinking I would look ridiculous in uniform. But I'm perfectly healthy, good-tempered, and amenable to discipline. I'm not suggesting I should harness myself to a gun and pull it up hills, but I am suggesting that I might sit in a hostel and do the mending and the catering, and keep a motherly eye on the girls. I like girls. I've had two daughters of my own, and I know how to talk to them.'

The A.T.S. shook their heads sadly. 'All you say is perfectly true,' they said, 'except about you looking ridiculous in uniform, because we think you'd look very nice.' (Lady B said afterwards that it must be true about the Recruiting Officers being chosen for their tact.) 'We'd love to have you, but the age-limit *is* forty-five, you know.'

Lady B bumbled sadly back in the bus, and called in at our house on the way home for comfort. Charles was so sorry for her that he gave her a glass of our last bottle of sherry, which Lady B accepted without demur, and that just shows how low her spirits were.

'Personally, I'm delighted that you were turned down,' said Charles, handing her a glass, 'though I think they were fools not to jump at you. You'd be worth your not inconsiderable weight in gold to any hostel, Lady B, darling. But, personally, I feel that this war is quite dreary enough down here without having you taken away from us.'

'Dear Charles!' said Lady B.

'Look at Henrietta brooding away in that chair,' said Charles. 'I know exactly what she's going to say.'

'What?' I said.

'That you want to go and make munitions.'

'Well, I do.'

'O.K.,' said Charles. 'Just find a woman to come and live in this house who is prepared to do the housekeeping, and look after me without getting on my nerves, and cook when Evensong★ is out, and fuss over Bill and the Linnet when they come home, and not mind if I don't speak when I'm tired, and do two hours in the garden every afternoon, and all without pay. Then you can go and get ill in a munitions factory whenever you like.' Charles recklessly poured himself out a second glass of sherry and tossed it off.

There was a long silence, and then suddenly, like a blinding flash, a Thought came into my head. 'Lady B!' I said.

Lady B and Charles stared at each other, and then Charles said in an awed voice: 'I can't imagine anything nicer.'

'Nor can I,' said Lady B, and he flew, as they say, into her arms and was folded to her breast.

'I hope you won't mind if I come home on leave sometimes,' I said bitterly.

But Lady B was frowning and pushing Charles away from her. 'Charles,' she said, 'I couldn't manage the garden. I'm a strong, healthy woman, but I could *not* do two hours gardening every afternoon.'

Charles looked at me doubtfully. 'Perhaps I'd better keep her,' he said, as though I were a new-born kitten.

★Evensong was one of Henrietta's two dailies. The other was called Matins.

18

He flew into her arms

So here I am, Robert, still in the Old Home, and practising the negative virtues of the wartime housekeeper. I'd rather be making munitions.

I have had a present. Two pairs of real silk stockings from Ceylon. When I opened the parcel I nearly fainted. They were so lovely I couldn't make up my mind to wear them, and the Linnet began to enquire about them in a very meaning sort of way, so that I took them out of my stocking drawer and locked them away in my desk for safety.

Then one day I did wear them. I always thought they would make their début at Bill's or the Linnet's wedding, or possibly the Peace Celebrations, but actually I wore them on the day our boiler burst, because by seven thirty p.m., with no drink in the house, civilian morale was running distinctly low, and silk stockings seemed the only things that could possibly raise it. Oh, the lovely, smooth, silky sheen of those stockings! I don't care what anybody says, lisle thread never gave a woman leg-assurance yet. When Charles came home, he found me swooning in an ecstasy.

'Look, Charles! Look at my lovely stockings!'

'Very nice. Your legs are your only claim to beauty, Henrietta.'

'But they're *real silk*, Charles!'

'Take care you don't get a ladder,' said Charles, in a killjoy sort of way.

'Don't be silly, Charles,' I said. 'How could I get a ladder just sitting in a chair?'

In the middle of dinner I laid down my knife and fork and stared across the table.

'What's the matter?' said Charles. 'Have you got a pain?'

Something had gone 'Ping!' at my knee and then run down my shin like the stroking of a gentle finger. But I had had my hour.

'What's the matter?' said Charles

Always your affectionate Childhood's Friend,

HENRIETTA

MY DEAR ROBERT   March 25, 1942

We are in the middle of Warships Week. There have already been two processions, and I wouldn't like to say how many raffle tickets I have bought and lost, but, as the Conductor says: 'Better to have bought and lost than never to have bought at all.'

Yesterday we had a Grand Variety Concert—in fact, two Grand Variety Concerts, because we had the same one twice, once in the afternoon and once in the evening. Lady B and I went in the afternoon, as she isn't allowed out at night because of her cough. As we settled ourselves into our plush tip-ups, we thought how nice it was to be sitting comfortably in the audience instead of working behind the scenes, as we generally do on these occasions. The hall was about half-full of our usual matinée audience, which enjoys itself in its own quiet way, and claps gently with its gloves on. Lady B and I, who have endured many such an audience from behind the footlights, took off our gloves and prepared to co-operate heart and soul with the performers but when Quartermaster Sergeant Black from the Camp came onto the stage and announced his intention of making us sing, I knew we were in for trouble.

' "The king was in his carnting-'ouse, Carnting aht his money," ' sang Quartermaster Sergeant Black, with appropriate gestures and, I am sorry to say, to a hymn-tune.

'Now just get on your feet and sing that,' said Quartermaster Sergeant Black genially.

There was a deathly silence and no one moved an inch.

'Come ON!' said the Quartermaster Sergeant, and I thought I detected a note of panic in his voice as he gazed down on our grey and nodding heads.

Lady B and I stood up. So did the Admiral, who must have felt that the honour of his home town was at stake. Following his good example, a few more people got sheepishly to their feet, including Colonel Simpkins, who stood stiffly to attention.

'Now, come ahn,' said the Quartermaster Sergeant, wisely ignoring the sitters. 'All together, and *with* gestures.'

' "The maid was in the garden hanging out the

clothes," ' we sang in quavering voices, and clawed obediently in the air above our heads.

'That's better. "When dahn came a blackbird," ' said the Quartermaster Sergeant encouragingly.

' "When down came a blackbird." ' We flapped our arms and bent our knees.

'If they *knew* how silly they looked!' said Mrs Whinebite in a loud voice just behind me.

'Dahn you go!' shouted the Quartermaster Sergeant. 'Lower dahn! There's only one lady going dahn properly.'

There was indeed. It was Lady B. Serene, and completely unselfconscious, she was sitting on her heels in the gangway, then her rheumatic ankle gave way, and she sat on the floor.

The Quartermaster Sergeant's turn provoked loud applause. Everybody, except the singers, had enjoyed every minute of it, but the Quartermaster Sergeant's bow was for Lady B alone.

After that came our Star Turn, a real professional singer, imported by the Conductor. At the end of her last delightful song the Admiral stepped forward and, with a courtly bow, presented her with a large bouquet of red carnations. There was a gasp from the audience, for we don't give those sort of bouquets down here, and little Mrs Simpkins whispered that they had cost a shilling each. Everybody who was near enough to hear this startling piece of information immediately began counting the blooms, and the singer, after a graceful little speech of thanks, offered her bouquet to be auctioned for the good of the cause.

For the second time that afternoon there was a deathly silence. I was just wondering whether I could possibly afford fifteen shillings out of the housekeeping when the singer said brightly: 'I bid three guineas.'

We sat in stunned silence which seemed to last for

hours, until it began to look as though our charming guest was going to have to pay for her own bouquet. Then the Conductor poked a white face out of the wings and croaked: 'Three pounds ten.'

'Three pounds fifteen,' said Lady B, who knew the Conductor couldn't afford it. I whispered that I would pay half and made a lightning decision to sell Aunt Eva's brooch.

'Five pounds,' said the singer, with a dazzling smile.

'Five guineas,' said Lady B faintly, and clutched my arm.

'Going, going, gone!' shouted the Admiral

'Going, going, gone!'

hurriedly, and banged on Mrs Savernack's hat as though it were an auctioneer's table.

The bouquet was handed to Lady B. Just for a moment we gazed upon its loveliness and sniffed its fragrance, and then she handed it back to the singer. Lady B does everything in style.

Lady B came back with me and we brewed ourselves some strong tea. After three cups each the milk gave out, but by that time we were feeling a good deal better. All the same, we decided that the next time they get up a Grand Variety Concert we're going to be in it, even if it is only noises off or pulling the curtain up and down.

Always your affectionate Childhood's Friend,

HENRIETTA

M Y DEAR ROBERT
     When I was taking Perry for his walk on the cliff
path yesterday, I met Mrs Savernack hurrying down the
hill, looking flushed and excited.

'I believe he's a spy,' she said, in a low and mysterious
voice.

'Who?'

'That old man over there,' said Mrs Savernack,
rolling a round and excited eye in the direction of a seat on
the edge of the cliff.

I looked and saw a
benevolent old gentleman
with a white moustache,
gazing out to sea. He was
wearing uniform. 'He looks
all right to me,' I said.

'He probably would,'
said Mrs Savernack,
with withering scorn.
'Anyone would look all
right to you unless they
were doing the goose-
step. Now, we'll walk
past slowly, and you must
take a good look at him.'

We walked past
slowly. 'Well?' said Mrs
Savernack.

A benevolent old gentleman

'Do people have
wound-stripes on their arms nowadays?' I said doubtfully.

'Of course they don't!' cried Mrs Savernack. 'And
they don't have rank-badges on their cuffs either, *or*
breeches and leggings. Now we'll go back again.'

We walked past again, even more slowly this time,
and the old gentleman began to look rather uncomfortable.

'His medal ribbons are in the wrong order!' hissed Mrs Savernack into my ear.

'How clever of you to know!' I said, with deep admiration.

Mrs Savernack gave me a pitying look. Just then the old gentleman took out his handkerchief and blew his nose with a loud, trumpeting sound. 'He's signalling to a submarine!' said Mrs Savernack, her voice shaking with excitement.

'Surely they'd never hear that under water,' I said.

'My good fool!' said Mrs Savernack. 'Now we'll go and sit down on the same seat, and draw him into conversation.'

'I shall laugh!'

'Don't be feeble, Henrietta.'

We approached the seat. The old gentleman, who had noticed our interest in him with increasing embarrassment, got up and went and sat on another seat, leaving his newspaper behind him. 'He reads the *Daily Telegraph*, anyway,' I said, 'and what could be more respectable than that?'

'It's a blind,' said Mrs Savernack, and began walking firmly up the hill towards him.

The old gentleman, with a hunted expression on his face, got to his feet and hurried down a side turning which leads to the Street. 'Run, Henrietta!' shouted Mrs Savernack. 'Take a short cut through the Admiral's garden. I'll hold the fort this end.'

The Admiral was digging a trench for beans as I rushed down the path. 'What on earth are you doing, Henrietta?' he said, leaning on his spade.

'It's a spy!'

'God bless my soul! Where?'

'Going down Sea Lane to the Street.'

The Admiral dropped his spade and padded down the

path behind me. At the bottom of the garden we leant over the wall and saw the spy approaching at a jog-trot. He was blowing a bit, and kept looking furtively behind him. 'Give me a hand,' I whispered to the Admiral, and put one leg over the wall. The Admiral, with a groan for his lumbago, lowered me into the road, where I fell at the spy's feet and twisted my ankle. The spy gave a yell, and began rushing back to the cliff path, but there Mrs Savernack barred the way like an avenging angel. With great spirit he turned in his tracks, and before I had time to get to my feet, ran past me down the road again and into the High Street, where he disappeared round the corner.

'The only thing to do now', said the Admiral, 'is to organise a systematic search,' and we decided to begin with the hotel.

When we arrived we went straight to the bar, and there, sitting on a high stool with his back to the door, drinking whisky and talking to one of the Lady Visitors, was our spy. We gave each other triumphant looks and crept in on tip-toe, and took our places at the bar just behind him, where we could hear what he was saying.

'And how is your granddaughter?' said the Lady Visitor.

'Prudence? She's all right,' said the spy, 'but she *will* use my clothing coupons.'

'What a shame!' said the Lady Visitor.

'And what she doesn't use her mother does,' said the spy. 'I lost five good suits in the Blitz, and now I'm reduced to wearing the uniform I had in the last war.'

'Three pink gins, please,' said the Admiral to the barman, in a low voice.

'You look very nice in it, Major,' said the Lady Visitor, who appeared to be one of those women who believe in making themselves pleasant at all costs.

'Funny place this,' said the spy. Then he leaned

forward in a confidential manner and said: 'Believe me or believe me not, I was chased—yes, positively chased—by two females on the cliff path this morning.'

'I can't believe it!' said the Lady Visitor.

'Fact, I assure you,' said the Major, twirling his moustache.

'Were they attractive?' said the Lady Visitor.

'Not a bit,' said the Major. 'And, what's more, they were old enough to know better.'

We swallowed our pink gins and crept out as

'I was chased by two females on the cliff path this morning'

silently as we had come in. As we got to the door we heard the Lady Visitor say: 'It must have been your uniform that attracted them, poor things.'

Always your affectionate Childhood's Friend,

HENRIETTA

May 6, 1942

M Y DEAR ROBERT
Spring is here, and I have started what Charles calls my rearguard action with the weeds. Daffodils are dancing and fluttering in a not inconsiderable, and definitely cold, breeze, and wood anemones rear their delicate heads, as people who write about the spring are so fond of saying.

Yet, in spite of the burgeoning and budding, life in your old home town is not as uneventful these days as I could wish it to be. A few days ago, in the middle of lunch, and without the slightest warning, things suddenly began to be very unpleasant indeed. After two tremendous Bangs and the rattle of machine-gun bullets, I slid gracefully under the dining-room table and cowered there until the enemy plane, after a few more Bangs, had roared over our chimney-pots and out to sea again.

I slid gracefully under the table

When I emerged, Charles was still eating his lunch. 'That gave you a turn,' he said with a grin.

'Yes.'

'Dirty swine,' said Charles, cutting himself another slice of bread.

'Yes.' I looked with distaste at the lunch I had been enjoying a few moments before.

'Eat up your food, Woman, eat up your food,' said Charles irritably.

'I don't really feel hungry now.'

'Can't work on an empty stomach,' said Charles. Then the telephone rang, and he said 'Ah,' and left the room, and a few minutes later I heard him drive away in his car.

If it was Hitler's idea to strike terror into the hearts of sleepy West Country folk, then the whole thing was a failure, because it has simply made everybody very angry indeed. Lady B came round that evening, quite pink with annoyance. 'I'm in such a temper,' she said.

Charles said he wished he could give her a little something, but there wasn't a drop in the cupboard.

When we asked Lady B if she had been upset by the Incidents, she said no, she had got under the piano and taken some of Fay's Dog Bromide mixture, which had worked wonders. Lady B said Fay had been quite unmoved by each shattering explosion, and had remained in her basket with a bored expression on her face.

'The people whose windows have been blown in are very scornful of the ones whose windows have not been blown in,' said Lady B. 'And the people whose doors and windows have been blown in are scornful of the people whose windows only have been blown in, and the people whose houses have been knocked down are scornful of everybody.'

'Snom bobbery is rife,' I said.

'What, dear?' said Lady B, peering at me anxiously.

'Snom bobbery.'

'She's probably suffering from shock,' said Charles to Lady B in a low tone.

We are all very proud of our home town, Robert. Nobody made a fuss and everything worked smoothly, rather to the disappointment of the Visitors who prophesied Muddles.

Mrs Savernack covered herself with glory by rushing into the garden and firing a shot-gun at the enemy plane.

She swears she scored a hit, and is now so flushed with success that she is trying to form a Women's Home Guard. She says she isn't going to ask me to join, because I wouldn't be any good.

The only person besides Lady B's Fay to be quite unmoved by the raid is our gardener, who is so deaf he never heard anything. When I told him about it he shook his head in a knowing way. 'Ar,' he said, 'her couldn't get me. I was in the old greenhouse.'

Always your affectionate Childhood's Friend,

HENRIETTA

MY DEAR ROBERT   June 3, 1942
Bill and the Linnet have both had a few days' leave. It was lovely having them at home together. Luckily the weather was beautiful, and they spent nearly all their time lying on the roof, playing the gramophone to each other.

Since they left home our gramophone records have got rather behind the times. There is nothing in the world as sad as an old dance tune and, once or twice, while shaking the mop out of the bathroom window and seeing them lying there in such pre-war abandon, I was moved almost to tears.

'What are you looking so miserable about?' shouted the Linnet.

'It's that tune about Smoke in My Eyes.'

'Gosh!' said Bill. 'It's so old you must almost have danced to it in your youth.'

'Oh, no, Bill,' said the Linnet seriously. 'Not as old as all *that*.'

Children say this sort of thing. They don't mean it unkindly . . .

Last week, when I was half-way up the cliff path, a sudden splutter overhead sent me headlong, like a rugby back, into the nearest doorway, which happened to be the entrance to the Men's Club. Colonel Simpkins, who happened to be coming out, stepped over me in some surprise.

'My dear Henrietta!' he said as he helped me to my feet.

I brushed the dust off my coat, feeling foolish.

'What *were* you doing?' said Colonel Simpkins. Just then there was another rattle overhead. Colonel Simpkins looked up and then smiled kindly at me. 'It's all right, you know; it's one of Ours,' he said, patting my arm. 'Not that it isn't a very sensible thing to do, Henrietta—very sensible indeed. We should always be ready for any emergency. By the way, I notice you are not carrying your gas-mask.'

'I'm sorry.'

'Keep it in your shopping basket, my dear. And now come and have some coffee.'

I remembered this kindness when we met next at Lady B's and poor Colonel Simpkins came most unexpectedly under attack.

Lady B is very indignant because only ninety-five people voted for equal compensation for women who get injured in air raids. The usually genial atmosphere of her little flat was charged with sex-antagonism when we all met there after church on Sunday morning to help her drink the bottle of sherry somebody had sent her for her birthday.

'I grudge every drop I pour into your glass,' said Lady B bitterly as she helped Colonel Simpkins.

Colonel Simpkins looked hurt. '*I* didn't vote against Equal Compensation,' he said, like a little boy who has been given an undeserved smack.

31

'Would you have voted for it?' said Lady B, standing over him like the Avenging Angel.

Colonel Simpkins exchanged a quick look with the Admiral and shuffled with his feet. 'It's all a matter of economics,' he said.

'Economics be damned!' said Lady B. 'My limbs are worth as much to me as yours are to you; more, in fact, because I'm a poor widow-woman in reduced circumstances, and if I had only one arm I wouldn't be able to cook my food, whereas if you had only one arm Mrs Simpkins would cook yours.'

'I might be left a widower one day. Who knows?' said Colonel Simpkins.

'What did you say, Alexander?' said little Mrs Simpkins, sitting up, her cheeks very pink.

'Life is very uncertain, my love,' mumbled the Colonel, for whom, I must say, my heart was bleeding.

'Well, if I were left a widow I know what I'd do,' said little Mrs Simpkins, clearly and unexpectedly. 'I'd move into a *much* smaller house, and I'd sell your roll-top desk.'

After that there was an awkward silence, broken at last by Faith, who was home for the week-end and who is sometimes tactful more by mistake than good management. She was standing beside the Admiral, and she put

'I really cannot see why my legs should be considered less valuable than the Admiral's!'

one leg forward and pulled her skirt up well above the knee. 'I really cannot see,' she said, 'why my legs should be considered less valuable than the Admiral's.'

There was another silence—an awed one this time, because, of course, Faith's legs are famous all over the West Country. I often wonder where she gets her silk stockings. Personally, I think that people with legs like hers ought to have them provided by the Government because they do so much for morale. After that, everybody cheered up. Lady B kissed Colonel Simpkins and said she hadn't meant to hurt his feelings, and Colonel Simpkins said that if Lady B lost an arm he would come and do her cooking himself, and Mrs Simpkins said, 'Come along home, you old Flirt.'

Afterwards, when Lady B and I were getting the lunch—for Charles was out with the Home Guard, and I had taken down my sausage roll to heat in Lady B's oven—I said to her, 'It's a good thing they've taken all the railings away, or you'd have been chained to them by now, shouting for Equal Compensation.' Lady B, who was making some mustard in a cup, chuckled. Then she looked up at me very seriously. 'No, I wouldn't, Henrietta,' she said. 'You can't do that sort of thing in wartime. That, of course, is where they score.'

'But there's nothing to stop you making a fuss after the war,' I said, 'and having processions with injured women wheeled in chairs.'

'Ah!' said Lady B. 'The poor souls!'

Always your affectionate Childhood's Friend,

HENRIETTA

33

M<small>Y</small> D<small>EAR</small> R<small>OBERT</small>   July 1, 1942
     On Tuesday I went to an orchestra practice. They are learning a piece which wants three little tiny Pings on the triangle, and I was chosen to deliver them.

'Your performance on the Nightingale during the Toy Symphony did nothing to justify my confidence in you as a triangle player,' said the Conductor unkindly, 'but I can't think of anybody else who can spare the time.'

'As a matter of fact, I can't spare the time myself, *actually*,' I said, but the Conductor ignored this remark.

I have often longed to attend a practice of what is known in this place as the Ork. Once or twice I have met the Conductor staggering away from the hall with a white face, followed by the flushed and twittering members of his orchestra, whose shaking legs can hardly carry them to the bun shop for cups of reviving coffee which will enable them to face the hill home.

At their yearly concert all is forgiven and forgotten, of course, and the Conductor, beaming with good nature, always waves the Ork to its feet to share in the applause. Afterwards they present him with a little speech of thanks and a fountain-pen, which he loses before the next concert. This saves them the trouble of thinking up some other idea. At the last concert, fountain-pens being off the market, they gave him six new-laid eggs. One of the second violins told me that when he thanked them there were tears in his eyes.

When I arrived at the hall, the orchestra was already assembled, making all the peculiar noises an orchestra does make when preparing to play.

'Late, Triangle!' said the Conductor, looking up from the score he was studying.

'I'm *not* late,' I said indignantly, for I had run all the way from our house in order to avoid this contingency. 'It's half a minute to eleven.'

'Your seat is at the back,' said the Conductor more kindly, 'next to the Double Bass. You don't come in at all in the first movement.'

Good. That would give me a whole movement, untrammelled by Pings, in which to study the Ork at work. I threaded my way with difficulty between the music-stands, and took my seat.

'Now,' said the Conductor, standing up, 'this is a lovely little work. It starts *presto forte-fortissimo*, and if it isn't played with gusto it isn't worth playing at all, so go to it for all you're worth. I shall count two in the bar. One—two——'

There was a crash of sound. The Ork had gone to it. Bow-arms were moving up and down like piston-rods, eyes were shining and hats askew. Could this really be sight-reading? The Ork was a marvel! The Double Bass beside me zoomed like thunder, and swaying to and fro, poked me in the cheek with its bow.

'Ow!' I said.

'I'm terribly sorry, Henrietta,' said the Double Bass.

The Conductor tapped his stand. 'What is all this disturbance at the back?' he said.

Poked me in the cheek

The Double Bass explained. 'Is it bleeding?' said the Conductor coldly.

'No.'

'Then don't make a fuss.'

'It might have been my eye,' I said reproachfully, and moved my chair, knocking over two cello cases as I did so.

The Conductor gave me a look and raised his hands. Off they went again *presto forte-fortissimo*, and then suddenly the music changed, and the first and second violins began a sad little tune in the minor key.

The Conductor tapped his stand. 'It has changed to the minor,' he said, looking at little Mrs Simpkins reproachfully.

'Yes, I do,' said little Mrs Simpkins, whose deafness has become a good deal worse lately. 'Very pretty indeed,' and she nodded and smiled.

The Conductor looked at her and sighed, and then they started again. Little Mrs Simpkins still played in the major key, and the Conductor stopped the Ork and went and shouted in her ear.

'Minor?' said little Mrs Simpkins. 'Just fancy!'

'We will now go back to letter L,' said the Conductor in a shaking voice, and they started. But whatever dear little Mrs Simpkins was playing—and she played with concentration and determination—it wasn't letter L.

'L!' shrieked the Conductor in a high voice. 'L!'

'I heard you,' said little Mrs Simpkins with dignity. 'M—M for Mummy.'

Her neighbour pointed out the place with her bow, and they started again. This time they got through to the end, and except for one little disturbance when the piece of velvet ribbon which Mrs Whinebite fastens round her neck with a press-stud came unpopped, and she knocked over three music-stands retrieving it, all went smoothly.

At the end, the Conductor mopped his face with his handkerchief. He looked rather white. 'We will now try the second movement,' he said, and I raised my triangle on high in readiness.

In triangle playing, if you have only three Pings in a

whole movement, and each Ping is separated from the next by at least eighty bars, and you aren't very good at reading music anyway, it is extremely difficult to Come In at the Right Time. The Conductor was sitting with his head in his hands, apparently weeping, by the time we had gone through the movement twice. After that I threw my music on the floor and trusted to Womanly Intuition and Memory. After the Double Bass had played three loud zooming notes I Pinged once; when one of the cellos turned round and gave me a Look, I Pinged a second time; and at the bit where little Mrs Simpkins began playing in flats instead of sharps, I Pinged for the third and last time. This was correct.

The Conductor said 'Good, Triangle!' and was I proud?

Always your affectionate Childhood's Friend,

HENRIETTA

July 15, 1942

MY DEAR ROBERT
When the war started I decided that anything in the way of relaxation and fun would be wrong, and I spent all my spare time weeding. The result of all this well-doing was that the war became a little wheel which went round and round in my head, and Lady B complained that I had got into the habit of frowning.

'What do you think about when you weed?' she said to me one day, as she sat and watched me busy among the onions.

'Well, all down that row I worried about the Linnet, and all down this one I'm worrying about Bill, and for the first three rows I worried about Libya, and for the next two our shipping losses, and——'

'Stop!' said Lady B. 'I am an old woman,' she went on, 'and nobody expects me to do more than knit, but I'd never take a knitting-needle in my hand again if I couldn't read at the same time and thus occupy my thoughts.'

'I wonder if one could read and weed?' I said.

'Of course you couldn't,' said Lady B. 'But it's time you snapped out of all this gloom, Henrietta. I think you'd better enter for the Bowling Tournament.'

'But I haven't played bowls since the war began.'

'That doesn't matter. I shall enter, too,' said Lady B recklessly. 'It will be unfortunate for our partners, but good for their self-control.'

Lady B and I entered for the Bowling Tournament. She drew the Admiral as her partner, and I drew Colonel Simpkins. Neither Colonel Simpkins nor the Admiral was pleased, but they generously decided to make the best of it. Lady B and I were, of course, delighted when we found we had drawn each other in the first round as opponents.

'It's a pity we have to play with four woods instead of two,' said Lady B, 'but we can soon trundle them down, and then have a nice chat.'

We trundled them down, and the people on the rinks on either side brought them back. The Admiral and Colonel Simpkins became rather red in the face, but said nothing.

'Now they've got the whole rink to themselves,' said Lady B, settling herself comfortably on a seat. 'I like your shirt, Henrietta. Where did you get it?'

'I made it out of some of Charles's old pyjamas. I used the legs for the sleeves.'

'My dear, how brilliant of you! I often wonder why men wear out the seats of their pyjamas the way they do. The collar's good.'

'I lined it.'

'Just pull up your jersey and let me see the back. Yes, it's definitely a success. And the colour is delightful. Charles must have looked sweet in it.'

'He did rather.'

A shadow fell across our knees, and we looked up to see the Admiral standing before us. 'Would it be too much to ask you ladies to pay a little attention to the game?' he said in a shaking voice.

'Well, Admiral darling,' said Lady B, 'our shots were so terribly bad they didn't really seem worth taking an interest in, if you know what I mean.'

'And your partners' play is a matter of indifference to you?'

'Of *course* not,' said Lady B, looking a little guilty. 'But we feel we can leave it all to you and Colonel Simpkins.'

The Admiral, who admires the Clinging Woman, was slightly mollified by this remark, as Lady B intended he should be. 'I suppose you wouldn't care to tell us from time to time which shot lies nearest the jack?' he said.

'But of course,' said Lady B, and she turned her attention, for the first time, to the rink, where eight woods were clustered neatly round the little white jack. 'It is your shot, Admiral dear, which is lying.'

'On the contrary, it is Colonel Simpkins's,' said the Admiral gloomily as he walked back to his place.

'I'm going to try very, very hard this time,' said Lady B to me in a low voice as she prepared for her next shot. Then she took a deep breath, shut her eyes, and sent her wood rolling down the green. It trundled gently along, curved round, and came to rest an inch from the jack. Lady B turned pale and clutched my arm. 'Henrietta! Look what I've done!' she said.

'Good shot!' yelled the Admiral.

'Oh, False Friend,' I said bitterly, and sent down one of my usual ones.

'Twenty-five yards short,' called Colonel Simpkins sadly.

Lady B, uplifted and inspired, made another brilliant shot which hit the jack and her wood was marked with a cross in white chalk.

Sent her wood rolling down the green

'I don't think I ever felt so proud in my life,' said Lady B, who had had triumphs in many European embassies.

'Look at all the people watching,' I said.

'Don't talk, please, Henrietta,' said Lady B in a remote way. 'I want to concentrate.'

Lady B and the Admiral won the Bowling Tournament. I went up to see them play their finals. A large crowd had assembled to watch. Lady B demanded perfect silence before she played each shot, and even asked a croquet player on a distant lawn not to make a clicking noise with the balls. Half-way through the game she had a brandy-and-soda brought out to her from the bar. Just before the end, inspiration left her and she began playing in her old and, to me, more attractive style. But by that time she and the Admiral were so far ahead they couldn't lose.

'I'm glad I've lost the Touch,' she said comfortably, coming to sit beside me. 'Being good at games takes all the fun out of them. My dear, *do* look at Mrs Whinebite's hat.'

Always your affectionate Childhood's Friend,

HENRIETTA

July 29, 1942

M<small>Y</small> D<small>EAR</small> R<small>OBERT</small> Mrs Savernack gave a party last week. We all brought our own food, and at the end there was a collection for the Canteen; but still, it was a party, and caused more excitement and gave more pleasure than anything that has happened here for a long time.

Mrs Savernack had her cousin, who is a real Cabinet Minister, staying with her, and she asked us all to come in our very best clothes, because of the Cabinet Minister's wife, who, Mrs Savernack said, is considered the Best Dressed Woman in London. You can imagine what a stir that caused but, of course, everybody was simply delighted to have the chance of wearing their very best, because there is a strong feeling down here that, unless particularly requested to do so by one's hostess, any form of Full Fig is unpatriotic.

Everybody rushed to get furs and feather boas out of moth-proof bags, and best frocks, which had been hanging between sheets for at least two years, were taken down and tenderly ironed.

Two days before the party I found Lady B in the Street, breathing wistfully on the glass window of Mathilde, our dress shop. 'You see that little black hat, Henrietta,' she said. 'Well, I want it for the party.'

'Are you sure?' I said, because Lady B always used to get her hats in Paris, and has vowed more than once that nothing less distinguished shall rest upon her head until every German has been driven from the sacred soil of France.

'Perfectly sure,' said Lady B firmly. 'I've only made a mistake over a hat once in my life, and that was when I was seventeen. It was made of pale-blue chiffon and had a pink rose under the brim. It was a terrible hat, but the first time I wore it Henry proposed to me. How odd it is that all the nicest men prefer a bad hat to a good one.'

I said, 'Yes.'

'I never thought I'd want to buy a hat out of our Street, but I want that little hat,' said Lady B, and she heaved a sigh which blurred quite a large patch on the shop window.

'Buy it,' I said.

Lady B turned anxious blue eyes on me. 'Do you think it would be helping Hitler?' she said in a low voice.

'It would help Mathilde's shop.'

'It is sometimes very difficult to know what is the Right Thing to do,' said Lady B, and she sighed again.

I rubbed the glass with my handkerchief, and we gazed once more in silence at the little black hat. Then I said: 'If you were to wire the brim of the hat you wore at the Thomson wedding, you could make it very like that one.'

'But I'd never get a quill that colour. I like the quill.'

'There are seagulls on the beach,' I said, 'and I have some coloured inks.'

The weather on the day of the party was lovely, and I thought I had never seen the Locals looking so smart and gay, but as soon as we caught sight of the Best Dressed Woman we realised that the one thing we had forgotten to do was to shorten our skirts. This cast a dowdy gloom over the beginning of the party, though people were able to throw it off later and enjoy themselves. Lady B looked a peach in the home-trimmed hat, and personally I thought she left the Best Dressed Woman at the post, but that may be because I had had a hand in the trimming.

I wore my black London coat, and my fox fur, mercifully preserved from the moth, and the hat I wore last time I lunched with you at the Savoy Grill. I remember you said you liked it, Robert, and so, according to Lady B, either you are not a nice man, or it is a bad hat. I kept thinking of this, and what fun that lunch had been, and how little real fun there is about these days, and what with these sad thoughts and my usual Party Panic, which attacks me on the doorstep, I arrived at Mrs Savernack's house in a very low state, and it was all I could do to get myself in at the front door.

The first thing I did at the party was to tread on a tomato sandwich which Colonel Simpkins had dropped on the floor, and grind it into the carpet with my heel. Drawing back with a cry of dismay, I bumped into the Conductor, who spilt his tea down the back of my coat. The Conductor mopped me up with his handkerchief, and we managed to scrape the tomato sandwich off the floor with the fire-shovel without either Mr or Mrs Savernack seeing.

'And this is our Doctor's Wife,' said Mrs Savernack, and I was propelled unwillingly into the Presence.

'I'm not. I'm Henrietta Brown,' I said.

'Yes?' they said, with gracious Government House smiles.

'At least, of course I *am* the Doctor's Wife, but I'm Henrietta Brown too, if you know what I mean. I always think it is rather depressing being called somebody's wife all the time.'

The Best Dressed Woman looked at me without sympathy. 'It has always made me very proud,' she said simply, and she and the Cabinet Minister exchanged a long, loving smile. After that there was a pause.

Feeling it was up to me to make a non-committal remark, I asked if they had seen the Savernacks' garden. They said they had, and that the fruit was magnificent.

I was propelled unwillingly into the Presence

I said: 'We're going to have a plumper bum crop this year.' Then Lady B came and led me away.

Mrs Whinebite arrived late, wearing the Mathilde model, and gave Lady B a very disagreeable look. Mrs Whinebite, who ought always to wear hats trimmed with raffia, and generally does, looked terrible in the Mathilde, and nobody but she and Lady B and I recognised it as a twin.

Always your affectionate Childhood's Friend,

HENRIETTA

August 12, 1942

M<small>Y DEAR ROBERT</small>
I have been having headaches. Evensong, who suffers dreadfully in her head, said they were nothing. I thought they were quite bad, but whenever I mentioned them to Charles, he said fretfully: 'For goodness' sake don't let's have Illness in the Home;' so at last I put on a hat and went and sat in his waiting-room with all the other patients. Even that wasn't a great success, because the patients said: 'You won't mind if I go before you, will you, because you can see dear Doctor Brown at any time, and I'm in such a hurry.' So that, in the end, I was the only one left, and Charles rushed in and said: 'I'm awfully sorry Henrietta, but I can't stop now. You must come another time.'

When the Linnet came home for some leave, I told her about my headaches. The Linnet, who is a sympathetic child, listened with attention, and when Charles came in she said, in a sort of nurse's voice: 'I think Mummy's got neurasthenia.'

'Then she'd better go and see Knox,' said Charles, in a relieved voice.

Knox is the eminent psychiatrist who heals the mentally unstable in our Cathedral City. Knox isn't his real name. We call him that because he is a Nervo specialist, from which you will gather, dear Robert, that this family is not yet cured of its habit of making poor jokes.*

The following Wednesday I was shown into the hushed stillness of Knox's exquisite waiting-room. I sat there in great contentment. I was a Patient at last. I hadn't enjoyed such a luxury for years.

A secretary with a face like a Madonna stole silently into the room. 'Will you come this way, Mrs Brown,' she

*Nervo and Knox were a pair of well-known music-hall comedians and members of the immensely popular Crazy Gang.

said, with a gentle smile, and I tip-toed into the Presence.

'My dear Henrietta,' said Knox. 'I am delighted to see you, but what brings you here?'

'I've got neurasthenia,' I said proudly.

'Dear me!' said Knox in his kindly way; 'and how have you managed to get that?'

'Do you think it might be the war?'

'It's a possibility.'

Knox's room was cool and dim, and the Patients' Chair a cradle of billowing comfort. After answering one or two sympathetic questions about the children, Matins, Evensong, and Shopping in the Street, my tongue was loosened and a torrent of words poured from my lips. Knox listened with the deepest attention. From time to time he made an attempt to say something himself, but I waved him aside and swept onwards, borne on the torrent of my own loquacity. I was a Patient with neurasthenia, and I had often heard Charles say that they did nothing but talk about themselves. Well, here was my chance. It might never occur again, and I was going to make the best of it.

At the end of an hour, I paused for breath, and Knox rang the bell and asked the secretary to bring me a glass of water.

'All you have told me is very interesting,' he said.

'Is it?' I said in a hoarse voice, and opened my mouth to begin again.

'Tell me,' said Knox quickly, 'do you ever have dreams?'

'Often.'

'Peculiar dreams?'

'Very peculiar. I once dreamt that I went to put something in the oven, and there, curled up on the bottom shelf, was a tiny little kangeroo. And another time I dreamt that Charles had grown a long, drooping moustache.'

'Nothing more peculiar than that?'

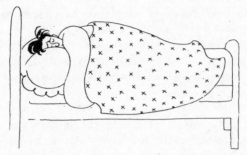

'I dreamt that Charles had grown a long, drooping moustache'

'If you don't think a kangaroo in the gas-cooker peculiar, I do.'

'Perhaps,' said Knox sadly, and wrote it down in his little book.

'She looks very flushed and excited, doesn't she?' said the Linnet, when I got home. 'Was it nice, darling?'

'It was *lovely*.'

'Have you got back to the Bee and the Pollen yet?' said Charles.

'I suppose you know you'll fall in love with the Doctor,' said the Linnet. 'They all do.'

'It's a very humiliating thought,' I said.

'Oh, I don't know,' said the Linnet. 'I think Knox is rather sweet.'

'He's very sweet. But having everything you say written down in a little book and typed out by the secretary afterwards is not my idea of a good love affair.'

'I see what you mean,' said the Linnet.

Always your affectionate Childhood's Friend,

HENRIETTA

P.S. My headaches have gone.

M Y DEAR ROBERT   September 9, 1942
      Every time I see one of those Fuel Target notices in
the paper a sort of film comes over my brain, but Charles
likes problems, and he spent the whole of what would have
been a free hour on Sunday afternoon working out how
much coal, gas, coke and electric light we would have to do
without this winter.

      After a lot of muttering he laid down his pencil and
said: 'That's easy. If we shut up the dining-room and put
one of those stoves in the drawing-room we ought to be all
right.'

      'Good.'

      'Of course, you must never light the gas-fire in your
bedroom, or use the electric iron, or the vacuum cleaner,
and I'm afraid you'll have to shut up your studio and bring
your work down to the drawing-room, and Matins and
Evensong must never have more than one burner alight at a
time on the gas-cooker; otherwise we can go on much as
usual.'

      'I see. I thought the Government said that if we saved
one lump of coal a day it would be enough.'

      'Did they say that?' said Charles. 'They can't have
meant it.'

      Charles now calls himself Herr Fuel Obermeister,
and has developed the irritating habit of poking his head
round the door of any room where I happen to be sitting
and switching off the light, leaving me in darkness. He says
that if we hit our Fuel Target he would like to be called Herr
Von Fuel Obermeister.

      I have become a sort of unofficial Fire-Watcher. I
can't be a proper one because, if Charles is out, there is
nobody to answer the telephone, but I have got a tin hat,
and a whistle with which to communicate with the Fire-
Watchers proper in the road below, and I walk about on the
flat roof outside my bedroom.

48

I was out there a few nights ago, admiring the moon on the sea and thinking that the hum of aeroplanes is quite the most disagreeable sound in the world, when I heard feet crunching on the gravel below. 'Who's there?' I said in a loud whisper, leaning over the parapet.

'It's Lady B,' said a voice out of the shadows. 'Can I come up?'

'Wait a minute and I'll come down and open the door.'

'Can't I come up the ladder?'

'Well, if you really want to——'

'Of course I want to,' said Lady B, and a minute later she was stepping nimbly over the parapet and onto the

She was stepping nimbly over the parapet

roof. By the light of the moon I could see she was wearing a neat siren suit and a tin hat.

'How nice you look,' I said.

'Nonsense, Henrietta!' said Lady B. 'An old woman of my age!' But I could hear she was pleased.

I got her another camp stool and we both sat down. 'If Winston can, then I can,' said Lady B.

'Can what?'

'Wear a siren suit.'

We sat in silence for a time, listening to the hum of aeroplanes overhead. Then I said: 'We used to have such fun on this roof once upon a time.'

'And so you will again,' said Lady B.

'All those boys and girls, so jolly, lying about in the sun enjoying themselves, and now——' I gulped, and Lady B put her hand on mine and gave it a little squeeze.

There was a distant Thump, and the roof shuddered gently beneath us. 'A long way off,' said Lady B.

'Near for some people.'

'We mustn't get gloomy, Henrietta,' said Lady B firmly. 'Sitting here in the dark one is inclined to but we mustn't. We've got to keep on sending great thought-waves of hope and cheer and confidence *rushing* round the world——' She made a sweeping gesture with her arm and knocked my tin hat over my nose. Almost at once we heard the splatter of machine-guns out to sea.

'We're after 'em!' I cried.

'Hurrah!' shouted Lady B. 'God save the King!'

There was a faint answering cheer from the Fire-Watchers in the road below, and soon afterwards the 'All Clear' sounded. We sat and listened in happy silence to the blissful sound. 'When the war is over,' I said, 'I'm going to have a gramophone record of the "All Clear", and put it on every time I feel blue.'

We tip-toed through my bedroom, where Charles was lying in an innocent and childlike sleep. Lady B leant over him, and with loving care tucked the bed clothes round his shoulders. In the kitchen we made ourselves some delicious tea, and then Lady B went home.

There are those who say that cups of tea in the night encourage sleep, but I am not one of them, and after I got back into bed I lay awake for a long time listening to Charles's gentle breathing and wishing I could have had a glass of milk. The birds were twittering before I finally dropped off. Almost at once the telephone rang. I could tell by the way Charles grunted into the receiver that he had to go out, and after a few muttered curses he bumbled out of bed and into his dressing-room.

When he came back the sun was shining in at the windows. He stood at the foot of my bed and said, 'You lucky little Thing, sleeping away there so peacefully all night, with nothing to disturb you.'

Always your affectionate Childhood's Friend,

HENRIETTA

September 23, 1942

MY DEAR ROBERT

We have all been to our Cathedral City to see *Hamlet*. One of the actors was a sort of cousin of Mrs Whinebite, and as the seats weren't going too well she rounded us up, like a cattle-rancher on the films, and herded us, lowing mournfully, up to the station and into the train.

'Is this Journey Really Necessary?' said Mrs Savernack, making a last bid for freedom.

'Yes,' said Mrs Whinebite firmly, and closed the carriage door on us while she went to buy tickets.

A good deal of the journey was spent in paying her back the money for our fares. Everybody borrowed change from everybody else, and even then it wouldn't come right, until a kindly clergyman in the corner offered nine pennies and a three-penny-bit in return for a shilling.

'Don't tell Mrs Whinebite,' said little Mrs Simpkins in a low voice, 'but I've forgotten what *Hamlet* is about.'

'It's about a young man called Hamlet,' said Colonel Simpkins helpfully.

'And a girl called Ophelia who goes mad,' said the Admiral.

'And a ghost,' said Lady B.

'And a queen called Gertrude who gets poisoned,' said the Conductor.

'And a king called Claudius who gets stabbed,' I said. 'And a young man called Laertes who gets killed in a duel, and an old man called Polonius who gets killed by mistake.'

Little Mrs Simpkins sighed. 'I remember now,' she said. 'Not a Bright Piece. I think they ought to try and put on something Bright in wartime, don't you?'

Robert, I am now middle-aged. 'Ever at my back I hear Time's wingèd chariot drawing near,' and many of the careless raptures of youth leave me with an unquickened pulse. But still, Robert, still I get the same old thrill as the curtain goes up. Charles says he has seen me sit, rapt, through a pierrot show on the beach, my hands damp with excitement; and though this isn't absolutely true, I *do* enjoy a play, and though Mrs Whinebite would never suspect it, the plays of William Shakespeare are my favourites, and of his plays the ones I 'did' at school and know well are the ones I like best of all.

The house lights lowered, and Lady B, who shares my passion for the drama, squeezed my hand, and the Curtain Went Up.

At the end of the first act Colonel Simpkins murmured something about not feeling well, and went out. The Admiral said he supposed he ought to see if the Old

Boy was all right, and went after him. Little Mrs Simpkins sighed again and said the Poor Ghost always depressed her, and Mrs Savernack said she supposed Hamlet must be over age, or he'd have been called up. Mrs Whinebite said, 'Was it Real or Feigned Madness?' and stared at us hungrily, each in turn, but nobody felt up to embarking on a discussion with her.

At the end, when the curtain came down on a stage strewn with corpses, I had sat so still that I had pins-and-needles in one foot and a crick in my neck. The Admiral and Colonel Simpkins were waiting for us on the steps outside. They both looked cheerful, and I guessed they had been to visit an Old School Chum who lives near the theatre.

'I've ordered tea at Treherne's,' said Mrs Whinebite.

'She thinks of everything, doesn't she?' said the Conductor, who had planned to take Lady B and me to his favourite hotel.

At the tea shop a large table had been prepared for us, as though we were a visiting hockey team, and Mrs Whinebite, wreathed in smiles, sat herself down behind the teapot, like a schoolmistress who has allowed discipline to relax for once.

'Poor little Ophelia!' said Lady B, passing a plate of thick bread and butter.

'The person I'm always so sorry for is Queen Gertrude,' I said.

'My dear Henrietta!' said Mrs Whinebite. 'She was an adulteress, and an incestuous one at that.'

'Oh dear, I do dislike those sort of words,' said little Mrs Simpkins.

'Well, I don't know,' I said, carried away by a subject to which I had given much thought. 'To begin with, I'm sure she didn't know her husband had been murdered, and then I can't help thinking she must have had rather a dreary life with Hamlet and his father. I mean to say, let's face it, Hamlet *was* a tiresome boy, though I dare say it was partly her fault for spoiling him. But if I'd heard Bill speaking to an old man like Hamlet spoke to Polonius, I'd have *spanked* him. And nobody could call Hamlet's father a jolly sort of man, though of course he may have been jollier before he became a ghost. I always think King Claudius must have been good fun. People with red hair often are.

He winked at me

Of course, he doesn't appear at his best in the play, biting his nails like that, but I expect he had plenty of charm and vitality really, and Gertrude fell for it, and who can blame her?' I paused for breath.

'Henrietta always likes to put forward an original point of view,' said Mrs Whinebite. 'Bless her!' she added viciously and I buried my scarlet face in my tea-cup.

'Fine play!' said Colonel Simpkins. 'I was only sorry I missed such a lot of it,' and he winked at me with the eye furthest from Mrs Whinebite.

Always your affectionate Childhood's Friend,

HENRIETTA

October 7, 1942

MY DEAR ROBERT

We have shut up our dining-room and put our dining-table and one of those stove things in the drawing-room. We consider that by doing this we have scored a bull's-eye in the Fuel Target, or at least an inner. Now I am making a little cosy corner in the linen cupboard, so that we shall be able to withdraw to better positions when Gwilym drives us from even the meagre comfort of our stove. What we shall do when he forbids the boiler fire as well, I do *not* know. Imagination boggles, as they say.

There has been a Salvage Drive going on here in an unused garage for the last fortnight. Charles and I made our big salvage effort several months ago, so our contributions this time have been rather puny, though Charles created a small stir by bringing some enormous tomes of out-of-date surgery, which he left on the pavement outside, the Salvage Authorities having locked up and gone away to a well-earned lunch. The books were full of unsuitable pictures, and quite a little crowd of Evacuees, on their way to school, gathered round to feast their eyes on them, until they were moved on by our policeman, who then began looking at them himself.

This afternoon I took down a watering-can with a hole in it, and found Mrs Savernack standing in front of one of the dumps looking wistfully at a mountain of pots, pans, kettles and what not.

'I could do with a lot of these things,' she said. 'That sweet little kettle, for instance.'

Began looking at them himself

'It's sure to have a hole in it.'

'But it could be mended, Henrietta,' she said eagerly. 'Look, it's only a tiny hole,' and she picked the kettle up, but dropped it guiltily when she saw the Admiral and Colonel Simpkins coming in at the garage door. As Chairman of the Urban District Council and Special Constable, they feel it their duty to visit the Dump every day.

'That's a nice watering-can,' said the Admiral.

'I brought it,' I said proudly.

'My dear Henrietta, you must be mad!' said the Admiral. 'It's only got one tiny hole, which could easily be mended.'

'That's just how I feel about that little kettle,' said Mrs Savernack, and they both snatched the objects of their desires off the Dump and held them up to the light.

It was then that Lady B came into the garage, staggering under the weight of an enormous pile of books. We were half-hidden from her by the pots and pans, and she tottered over to the Paper Dump without having seen us.

We looked at each other with concern, for Lady B loves her books, and when she gave up her house and moved into her tiny flat they were the only luxury she allowed herself to take with her. We tip-toed round to the other side of our tin mountain, and there she was, tight-lipped, throwing one precious volume after another onto the Paper Dump. I saw her beloved Trollopes hurtling through the air, followed by the Shaws, and as each old and valued friend landed with a melancholy plop on the sacrificial altar, Lady B muttered, 'Damn Hitler!'

Colonel Simpkins, who was deeply moved by this little scene, surprised us by inviting us all to tea with him at the hotel. Lady B said she must put on her best hat first, and we waited outside her flat while she made the necessary change.

As we trooped into the hotel lounge, I heard one of the Visitors say, 'Who are these people?'

'Locals,' said her friend.

'My dear,' said the first Visitor, 'I'm told they never do a tap, and spend the *whole* day playing bridge.'

'Four more A.R.P.s called up this month,' said the

Admiral. 'The women will have to come forward.'

'I thought you used to say the Woman's Place was the Home,' said Lady B.

'So it is, in peacetime,' said the Admiral. 'War is different.'

'Poor women!' I said.

'They ought to be proud to come at their Country's Need,' said Colonel Simpkins, looking at me very sternly.

'They are,' I said. 'Only they must get rather sick of being mucked about.'

'What a disgusting expression,' said Mrs Savernack.

'What Henrietta means,' said Lady B, 'is that one day women are being told that their place is the Home, and the next minute they have to man the guns.'

'And if they get their legs blown off, it's supposed to matter less to them than it does to a man,' I said.

'And as soon as they've got used to manning the guns, the war will end, and they'll be told their place is the Home again,' said Lady B.

'Bad luck, of course,' said the Admiral, 'but War is War.'

'I wonder how men would like it if they were whipped out of the Navy and Stock Exchange and things of that kind, and made to push babies about in prams all day,' said Lady B, who was warming to her subject.

'Of course, I always maintain, that Woman's Place is *not* the Home,' said Mrs Savernack.

'Oh, yes, it is,' said Lady B. 'And most of the nice, sensible women were in homes before the war, and too busy to come out of them; and that's why we have so few women Members of Parliament. But 'pon my word, if the country had been ruled by women for the last twenty years, they couldn't have made a worse mess of it than the men. When peace comes, I really think we'll have to put the men to pram-pushing, and see what we can do about it.'

The Admiral mopped his brow. 'You weren't a Suffragette before the last war by any chance, were you?' he said.

Lady B twinkled at him. 'We were abroad at the time,' she said, 'but I'd have liked to be one.'

'She'd have chained herself to the railings,' said Colonel Simpkins, looking helplessly at the Admiral.

'I certainly would,' said Lady B.

Always your affectionate Childhood's Friend,

HENRIETTA

November 18, 1942

MY DEAR ROBERT
Our wine merchant, who is always rather kind to us because he used to play cricket with Charles's father, was kinder than usual this month and sent us an extra bottle of gin, so we asked Faith, who is home on leave, and the Conductor to drinks on Saturday night. Lady B came too, and it was quite pre-war and the greatest fun.

In the middle the Linnet, who had got a day off, walked in looking so radiant that I knew something must have happened. 'You'd better tell us straight away,' I said as she stood there smiling and blinking in the light.

'Who is it?' said Charles sternly.

'Philip,' said the Linnet, and there was a silence, because nobody could think of any adequate reason why she shouldn't be engaged to Philip, who is very nice.

'He hasn't asked my consent yet,' said Charles, who has confided to me more than once that he was looking forward to throwing his weight about over his daughter's engagement.

'Sweetie Pie, he's coming to see you as soon as he can get some leave,' said the Linnet soothingly.

'Mind you, there's to be no question of an engagement until I have interviewed this young man,' said Charles pompously.

'Don't be tiresome, Charles,' said Lady B, who loves a romance. 'Come here, Linnet, and let me kiss you.'

The Linnet was folded to that warm and loving bosom, and I stood, with the cocktail-shaker in my hand, prodding gently at my emotions as one prods with one's tongue at a tooth which may begin aching any minute. I was pleased and surprised to find that, contrary to all I had been told of a Mother's Heart on such occasions, mine was like a Singing Bird, and my eyes filled with joyful tears, so that I overfilled the Conductor's glass and it all ran down over his legs.

'Look what you're doing!' yelled Charles, and the Conductor sucked his knee

The Linnet was folded to that warm and loving bosom

so that not a drop of the precious fluid should be wasted.

You have always said, Robert, that there is only one thing more depressing than a woman talking about her daughter's wedding, and that is a woman talking about her daughter's engagement, so I will lay off the Linnet and begin on Faith, who is neither my daughter nor engaged, though, of course, we all hope she will fix things up with the Conductor some day.

After all the excitement about the Linnet had died down we found ourselves in a very emotional state, and the Conductor fixed Faith with a mournful gaze so full of dog-like devotion that Charles cried, 'Why, in God's name, don't you marry the man, Faith, and put him out of his misery?'

'I don't know,' said Faith, opening her blue eyes very wide.

'Well, it's time you did,' said Charles crisply.

'Don't be harsh with her, Charles,' said the Conductor.

'He isn't being harsh!' cried Faith. 'He couldn't be! Could you, my Angel Kiss?' and she threw herself into Charles's arms.

The Conductor winced, and I wondered whether it would ease the situation if I were to throw myself into his arms. I looked at Lady B. The same thought, I could see, had crossed her mind but, catching my eye, she gave an almost imperceptible shake of the head. The Linnet, who was the only person present who could have made this gesture with success, was lost in a happy dream, so the only thing was for Lady B to get up and say it was time to go home.

I think the Conductor must have been upset, because he left his mackintosh behind. He rang up later to ask if it were there, and we said yes, hanging on the banisters, and after dinner he and Faith came round to fetch it.

'This isn't my mackintosh,' said the Conductor.

We said it wasn't ours either. Then Charles said might it be Lady B's? And I said no, Lady B's was a grey one.

'Well, I must say it's all very *peculiar*,' said Faith, looking at us in a meaningful sort of way.

'I hope you aren't accusing us of stealing the mackintosh?' I said.

'Not stealing exactly,' said Faith, 'but, of course, with the Linnet getting married you're bound to be short of coupons.'

'Well, I'm damned!' said Charles and shut the front

door behind them more loudly than was strictly necessary.

Later the Conductor rang up to say the coat was his landlady's, which he had brought along by mistake, and his own was at home, hanging in the hall. Charles thinks the incident may have drawn them closer together.

Always your affectionate Childhood's Friend,

HENRIETTA

January 13, 1943

M Y DEAR ROBERT
Charles and I spent a very quiet Christmas without the children. We gave each other a book about Nelson which we both wanted to read, but our most exciting present was a sort of felt glove for putting coal on the fire. Its underside is black, to match the coal, and the top a sprightly green decorated with little felt flowers.

Charles and I were delighted with it because, ever since our home life became darkened by the Fuel Target, it has been our frugal custom to put coal on the fire with our fingers. Each time Charles finishes this domestic duty, he rises to his feet, with his blackened fingers held stiffly before him, opens the door with his elbow, stumps upstairs to the bathroom, turns on the basin tap with his other elbow, and has a good wash. I, who have not been trained in such aseptic methods, and am not as clean as Charles, anyway, and often in more of a hurry, have other ways.

'Look, Charles,' I said. 'Black underneath, so as not to show the dirt.'

'It's a *lovely* present,' said Charles, slipping his hand inside.

'Now you won't have to open the door with your elbow any more.'

'And you won't have to wipe your fingers on your knickers, Henrietta.'

'They are black knickers, Charles.'

'And I have *not* forgotten the occasion,' went on Charles sternly, 'when I happened to be standing near, and you wiped your fingers on the trousers of my dark-blue suit.'

'Charles, this is Christmas Day!'

'Very well,' said Charles. 'We'll say no more about it.'

It was Christmas afternoon. The fire, thanks to the glove, was blazing merrily. Perry was asleep in his basket, the telephone was mercifully silent and Charles and I, who had lunched lightly off soup, cheese and celery, reminded each other with pleasure of our friends who, after turkey and plum pudding, would by now be feeling stodged and flushed.

'That glove,' said Charles, after a long silence, 'ought to hang on a nail.'

It was the thought I had been keeping at bay for a long time. No housewife likes to be reminded of such things on a Christmas afternoon. Directly she hears the word 'nail,' her mind flies to the tool box, and she remembers, with a twinge of conscience, that it needs tidying, and that all the nails are rattling around on the bottom, instead of lying neatly in the empty cigar-box marked 'NAILS', which, for some reason, is full of picture-wire. From this unpleasant thought her mind leaps to the possibility that there are no nails. Did she not tell the gardener last week that he could take all he wanted to mend the greenhouse door? No gardener has ever been known to return a nail from whence it came, and the housewife feels pretty sure that, if there are any nails left, they are on the shelf in the greenhouse with the seed catalogues and the secateurs. How terrible, on a cosy Christmas afternoon, to have to walk down the garden in the rain to look on the shelf in the greenhouse! Surely there must be *one* nail left, leading a care-free rolling life at the bottom of the tool box? Or perhaps a tin-tack? No, the tin-tacks were all used up on the blackout in the bathroom . . .

'If you aren't going to read that book about Nelson, you might let me have it,' said Charles, and I handed it over.

It would be so simple to get up from one's chair, go to the tool box in the scullery, find a nail, take the hammer in hand and with three deft strokes assure for oneself a sense of smugness and well-being for many months to come.

But could one be absolutely sure of the hammer being in the tool box? Was it not Matins who only yesterday took it for the linoleum in the hall? In which case, of course, it would now be in the kitchen drawer, or possibly on the dresser.

Charles laid down the book about Nelson. 'If you will bring me the hammer and a nail I will do the job,' he said generously.

'If you'll bring *me* the hammer and a nail I'll do the job myself,' I said. 'In the meantime, if you aren't reading that book about Nelson . . .'

No man likes to hear his wife talk that way, and Charles looked hurt.

'I am reading it,' he said; 'and, anyway, I don't know where the hammer and nails are kept.'

At four o'clock Lady B arrived to spend the rest of Christmas Day with us. The telephone woke up and rang for Charles, and I went to put the kettle on for tea, so we left her in front of the fire, looking at the Nelson book.

When we got back, she said: 'What a lovely glove for the coal! I've nailed it up for you.'

Charles and I stared at her and at the glove, hanging so neatly beside the fire-place.

'Where did you find the hammer and the nails?' we said.

'In your tool box, in the scullery, of course,' said Lady B, opening her eyes very wide.

'You're wonderful!' I said, and I gave her a hug because she hadn't said that the tool box wanted tidying, and most women would.

Charles produced a bottle of claret from the cellar, which I am beginning to think is like the widow's cruse, and, after our frugal meal, we sat and talked.

'I've nailed it up for you'

Lady B says she can *just* bear wearing woollen stockings during the day, but in the evening they rise up and choke her, and she has to go upstairs and change into a pair of silk ones with ladders.

Always your affectionate Childhood's Friend,

HENRIETTA

MY DEAR ROBERT

There was a time when I preferred summer to winter. Feeling the cold as I do, the approach of January, February and March used to fill me with dread; and soon after Christmas, when the east winds began to blow, I would get what Charles calls my 'sick monkey look', and, wrapped in misery and shawls, remain, like the hibernating toad, in a state of suspended animation until the first really warm spring day recalled me to life.

But all that is changed now. Since I took to gardening, winter has become my favourite season. You may well ask why, Robert, and the answer is easy to give. It is because in winter there are no weeds. Even my enemy, the bindweed, withers off at the top into thin, dead strings, and, though it is still lurking underground in all its coiling horror, a little concentrated wishful thinking easily persuades me that it is gone for ever. This excites in me a frenzy of enthusiastic tidying, and the edges of the grass are cut, the gravel paths raked and, if a dead leaf dares to lie for one instant upon the lawn, it is whisked away and plunged into a large pit dug for the purpose, where it lies rotting with its fellows, and is transformed in course of time, we hope, into rich leaf mould.

When I persuaded Charles, who hates the garden and looks at it as seldom as possible, to inspect what I had done, he said it was so neat it reminded him of an operating theatre. Charles has often been heard to remark that it would save his money and my time if the whole thing were laid down in concrete.

'What would we do with such a great expanse of concrete?' I said to him on one occasion, when he had made this shattering assertion.

But Charles always has an answer. 'We would invite our friends to roller-skate on it,' he said.

With no weeds rearing their ugly heads, and the

autumn leaves safely tucked away in their pit, I am hard put to it to find employment in the garden just now. To rest from my labours I do not dare, for muscles must be kept strong and lumbar regions supple against the Spring Offensive. Just lately I have been making a brick path. This is fascinating work, up to a point, the point being where a whole brick has to be made into a half-brick. When proper bricklayers do this it looks easy. They just take the little trowel-thing that they spread mortar with, and give the brick a tap, and it falls neatly into two pieces. I tried tapping my brick with an ordinary gardening trowel, and nothing happened at all. Then our gardener came along. Our gardener and I, like King James of the great Sir Walter, think but Rawley of each other, and never ask each other's advice if we can possibly avoid it. The gardener, with a pitying smile, stood and watched me stagger with bricks from one end of the terrace to the other. Watching me garden is one of our gardener's favourite pastimes. He never seems to

The gardener, with a pitying smile, stood and watched me

tire of it, and spends hours out of the two days he is supposed to work for us engaged in this happy pursuit.

'Layin' bricks?' he said kindly, after about ten minutes.

'Yes.'

'Yu knows as how you mustn't never lay one whole brick 'long side 'nother whole brick, don't ee?'

'Of course.'

'Do ee know the way to split bricks?'

'Er—yes, I think so.'

'I'll show ee!' cried the gardener, delighted at my hesitation; and, dropping the hoe which he carries about with him as a sort of badge of office, he seized my brick, gave it a sharp tap with the trowel, and it fell in half.

'That's how 'tis done,' he said conceitedly.

I was very much annoyed by this sudden display of efficiency, and as soon as he had gone, I took the trowel and gave my brick a tremendous whack with it. Nothing happened, so I turned it over and tried the other side. Again nothing happened, except that a small piece chipped off and flew into my eye. By this time my blood was up, and I went and got the axe out of the tool-shed. Laying the brick down, I raised the axe above my head with both hands, and delivered a stunning blow, which might have been effective if it had not missed its mark and buried itself deeply in the ground.

'What *are* you doing, Henrietta?' said Lady B, who often walks into our garden in the afternoons to give me a word of cheer.

'Breaking bricks in half,' I said breathlessly.

'But, my dear, that's quite the wrong way to do it,' said Lady B. 'All you have to do is just to tap it with a trowel, like this.'

'Exactly,' I said, after she had made several abortive attempts, and I returned to my brick with redoubled fury. I whacked and banged and scored several directs hits, as well as some near misses, while Lady B uttered little cries of encouragement, but apart from the fact that we both got little chips in our eyes, and the brick soon ceased to look like a brick, nothing happened. Then the axe broke, and we went indoors and had tea.

Next day I got a professional bricklayer to come and finish the job for me. It took him about ten minutes.

When the gardener came again, he inspected the new path. I could see he was disgusted to find the job so neatly done. 'Woman's work,' he said scornfully, trying to raise a brick with the toe of his boot.

'Looks nice, doesn't it?' I said smugly.

'Where be axe gone to?' said the gardener suspiciously.

'Gone to be sharpened,' I said.

Always your affectionate Childhood's Friend,

HENRIETTA

M Y DEAR ROBERT   14 April, 1943
Now the evenings are longer, Lady B often comes up to our house for a chat after dinner. She is the only person Charles doesn't mind coming to the house at that time, because he knows he can go on reading the paper and she won't mind if he grunts. Indeed, Lady B has remarked more than once that she likes Charles's grunts, as they remind her of her own happy married life. She even goes so far as to say that she understands what they mean, but I think that is just vain boasting on her part.

The night before last she arrived with her knitting. 'If you get up, Charles, I'll never come here again,' she said, and Charles, with a thankful sigh, abandoned the half-hearted attempt he was making to struggle out of his chair, and disappeared behind *The Times*.

'There's your chair,' I said.

Lady B hitched up her skirt at the back and sat down carefully. 'One of the major troubles of my life just now,' she said earnestly, 'is trying to keep my two good skirts from bulging at the back.'

'I always wear a very, very old one in the house.'

'So I see,' said Lady B. 'What has made you so tired to-night, Henrietta?', for I was playing patience, and Lady B knows that I only do that when I am too exhausted to do anything else.

'Bindweed.'

'Ah! I hope you admired me in the "Wings for Victory" procession?'

'I thought you looked very fine, and I was glad to see that you had the courage to carry an umbrella.'

'People were rather unkind about it at first, but they were glad to shelter under it when that shower began. Henrietta, I don't want to interfere with your patience, but if you don't put that Knave on the Queen I shall go raving mad.'

I put the Knave on the Queen. 'The people they really ought to have in processions, and when the great Peace Procession comes I hope they will, are the Shoppers.'

There was a grunt from Charles and *The Times* quivered slightly. 'Charles and I couldn't agree with you more,' said Lady B. 'Shopping Baskets in one hand and Ration Books in the other they would walk right at the end of the procession, in single file, like a queue and they'd get a rousing cheer if nobody else did.'

There was another grunt from Charles who had spent last Saturday morning shopping with me in our Cathedral City. Charles wanted to order a tweed jacket before they went all comic, and I wanted a paint brush. We found our city very much changed. The streets are crowded as they always have been, but now, instead of strolling in the road and holding up the traffic, the people hurry along the pavements with set expressions on their faces, while the motors whizz up and down at such a rate that Charles and I clung to each other on the kerb and feared to launch away. There was hardly a Devon voice to be heard. Even in Charles's tailors we detected an irreverent note, and the Dignitary who used to serve us was no longer there.

'Where is Mr Clement?' we asked.

'Gone,' said the New Man, with a grin. 'He was seventy-eight, you know.'

Charles was so annoyed at this levity that he refused the only cheerful check tweed left in the shop and chose a dull, countyish cloth into which little flecks of red and yellow were woven without enlivening its appearance in any way.

'Better take your measurements again,' said the New Man. 'Most people have lost a bit round the tummy.'

'Tummy,' indeed! The very walls shuddered, while Charles, pale with disgust, suffered his waistcoat to be pulled up and the tape passed around his waist.

The tape passed around his waist

'We haven't any No. 4 paint brushes left,' said the Girl in Artists' Materials, who was also new and obviously considered herself Queen of the May. 'See for yourself.' And yawning a little she pulled open the paint brush drawer. Inside were two paint brushes. One could have been used for painting a house and the other for a very small miniature.

Charles and I greeted our old friend the waiter with tears of recognition, but there wasn't any lunch. Yesterday had been market day and there wasn't anything left. Sadly we stepped into the street and threaded our patient way to a More Expensive House. 'Could we have lunch?' we asked meekly, standing on the mat. Authority looked us up and down. Yes, it thought it might manage something.

Joyfully and effusively we expressed our thanks and fought our way to the bar, which was full of people we didn't know. There, over drinks which called themselves Gin and French, we cheered up a little. 'I think it is probably what is called Hooch,' said Charles, 'and will make us blind.' When I asked him which sort of blind he said, 'Both sorts.'

Then we saw Geoffrey. Of course, it isn't fair to judge *anybody's* figure in battle-dress. Otherwise he looked just the same.

'I suppose you are drunk with power now you are a Second Lieutenant,' I said. Then Charles kicked me under the table, and I noticed that it wasn't a pip on Geoffrey's shoulder but a crown.

This created such an Atmosphere that I would have been glad to leave but Charles said No, we had ordered our grill and we would wait for it. And wait for it we did.

When it arrived at last it was quite good. 'So it ought to be,' said Charles. 'At that price.' Then I threw discretion to the winds and had some rice pudding, but it tasted of fish, and we came away.

'Who are all these people?' said Charles plaintively, after he had been pushed off the pavement and into the gutter for the third time. But we reached the garage at last, and scrambled into our car like shipwrecked mariners into a lifeboat. 'It used to be fun,' said Charles sadly, and we drove away.

In the Cathedral Close there was a poster announcing music for that afternoon. I told Charles I would find my own way home, and joined the queue. Queueing is such a habit now that it holds no terrors and it didn't seem long till we were all inside and the music began.

Here was something which had not changed. Beauty, and peace, and comfort, and the grey walls of our beloved cathedral taking up the sound as they had taken up the prayers and songs of centuries to give them back to bewildered worshippers in kindly blessing. Many people were in tears.

I dropped in at Lady B's on the way home to tell her about the music. While I was there a very small girl arrived at the front door. 'Please,' she said, 'will you buy a ticket for our Fashion Play?'

'Your what, dear?' said Lady B.

'Fashion Play. In the church.'

Lady B. opened her bag. 'You haven't got that *absolutely* right,' she said, 'but I'd like to buy a ticket.'

Always your affectionate Childhood's Friend,

HENRIETTA

M Y DEAR ROBERT   June 16, 1943

The Conductor and Faith are married. At the last moment Faith developed Qualms, Doubts and Fears. First she said she wanted to be married in a Registry Office, and when the Conductor stoutly refused to be a party to such heathenish antics, she said she couldn't be married in our church, because the face of a centurion in the East window always reminded her of her first husband. Lady B and I thought this a bit far-fetched, but in the end it was arranged that they should be married in a village church five miles away.

'It's just like you, Faith, to make things as difficult as possible for everybody,' said Charles crossly. 'I thought I should be able to pop into the hospital on the way to the church, and now I've got to waste the whole afternoon driving miles into the country.'

Faith's beautiful eyes filled with tears. 'Of course, if you don't *want* to give me away, Charles,' she said.

'About flowers——' said Lady B.

'I thought delphiniums,' said Faith. 'You see, blue is my colour. Two huge bunches of mixed blues would look lovely against those whitewashed walls, don't you think? I've hired some blue carpet.'

It struck me that for somebody who was suffering from Qualms, Doubts and Fears, Faith had got everything very clearly arranged, and I began to understand why she had insisted on the village church.

'I shall feel so awful walking up the aisle all alone,' said Faith. 'I was wondering, darling Henrietta, whether you would wear your long blue frock—it's such a lovely cut—and be my Matron of Honour? You see, I'm wearing powder blue, and a sombre touch is just what is needed.'

'No, Faith,' I said. 'I love you very much, but I'm not going to be a Sombre Touch at your wedding. Besides, you won't be alone—you'll have Charles.'

Charles said suddenly, 'What am I going to wear?' and there was a horrible silence, because he always borrows the Conductor's wedding garments when he has to dress up.

'You can have The Suit, Old Boy,' said the Conductor, too happy to be worried by such trifles.

'Don't be silly,' said Lady B. 'You can't marry Faith in a pair of corduroy trousers.'

'He looks sweet in them,' said Faith, 'but they wouldn't go with my Powder Blue.'

'We might do a quick change in the vestry,' said Charles. 'Then I could walk up the aisle in The Suit, and you could walk down in it, and the Squander Bug would fall dead in the porch.' But Lady B said Charles must wear his Best Blue, and that was the end of that.

I started very early for Faith's wedding because I hadn't been on a bicycle since the first year of the war, when I fell off, and I'd promised Faith to give the delphiniums a final touch before the service. As I wobbled painfully past the station the passengers from the London train were just coming out, and suddenly I saw the Awful Dan.*

One of the funny things about bicycling is that whenever you particularly don't want to run into something you always do, and I found myself bearing down upon Dan at a breakneck speed. 'Get out of my way, Dan!' I shouted, but Dan stood fair and square in my path and took firm hold of the handlebars, so that I shot forward and my face hit his chest, leaving a patch of powder on his uniform.

'Not for the first time,' said Dan, beating his chest so that quite a cloud of powder rose in the air.

'I don't doubt it,' I said coldly, for I had taken trouble with my face.

'You still look a good deal nicer than usual,' said Dan kindly. Then he peered closely at me and began to laugh. 'You've got mascara on your eyelashes, you funny little thing,' he said.

'I'm going to a wedding,' I said. 'Faith's wedding, as a matter of fact,' and I looked to see him wince.

'Good!' said Dan. 'I like weddings.'

---

*An ex-suitor of Faith's whose unexpected release from an Italian prisoner-of-war camp a few weeks previously had given the Conductor (and perhaps Faith too) some sleepless nights.

He wanted to ride my bicycle and make me sit on the handlebars, but I refused to do this, so he borrowed one from the porter and we set off together, Dan with one hand between my shoulders pushing me up the hills, so that we arrived at the village church in no time. After I had looked at the delphiniums, which were perfect, we went and sat in a sunny corner of the churchyard.

'By the way, who is Faith marrying?' said Dan. 'That Conductor chap, I suppose?'

I nodded. 'You aren't sad are you?' I said.

'Sad? Me?' said Dan. 'Why?'

'I just wondered,' I said. 'She's wearing powder blue.'

'She would,' said Dan.

Nearly everybody came to Faith's wedding on bicycles. The hedge outside the village church was stacked with them, and a woman in one of the cottages opposite gave up her front room for people to tidy themselves up in before going into the church. Colonel Simpkins came in his little pony cart, which he hitched to the vicarage gate, and the pony ate most of the vicar's hedge during the service.

The Conductor, who had never had the chance of appearing in The Suit before because Charles was always wearing it, astonished us all by his magnificent appearance. Faith looked quite exquisite. Her eyes matched the delphiniums, and just the right Sombre Touch was provided by Charles's blue suit. Everybody was moved by the sight, and I felt the tears coming into my own eyes. It is a mistake to cry, even a little bit, when you have mascara on your eyelashes. In less than a minute I was in agony and the tears were pouring down my cheeks. Dan looked at me and then handed me a large, clean, white pocket handkerchief.

The reception, which was held in Faith's house, was a tremendous success. There was no champagne, but a sort of Cup, which had been brewed by Charles, produced a very hilarious spirit among the guests, and everybody, including Dan, kissed the bride a great many times.

'What were you crying about in church?' said Mrs Savernack to me, rather spitefully. 'The Conductor says he's going to keep on the choir.'

'She was wishing she'd married me instead of Charles,' said Dan.

'I quite enjoyed the wedding,' said Charles to me that evening. 'What did you think of the Brew?'

'Excellent, and extremely potent. I enjoyed the wedding too. Dan shoved me up the hills and we sat in the churchyard and had a flirtation.'

Brewed by Charles

'Dan would flirt with anything,' said Charles. Then he yawned and opened *The Times*.

Always your affectionate Childhood's Friend,

HENRIETTA

June 30, 1943

MY DEAR ROBERT
A Queen of the W.V.S. came down to talk to us one day last week. I met Lady B hurrying down the Street that morning, so as to get her shopping done early before the meeting, and we walked along together. It was an

unpleasant, cold, wet day, and everybody we met looked worried and hurried.

'The Shopping Face seems to have got worse lately,' said Lady B, after Mrs Savernack had passed us; muttering, with a sort of gardening-basket-wheelbarrow pushed before her.

I glanced in the large mirror which our grocer so kindly keeps in his window for the use of lady customers, and shuddered.

'I don't mind waiting my turn,' said Mrs Admiral, white with rage, coming out of the grocer's at that moment, 'but one day when some woman pushes her way forward, I shall Strike Her!'

'But you *promised* me liver,' wailed little Mrs Simpkins in the butcher's.

'No liver today, Madam,' said Mr Bones, that patient man.

'Kidneys?'

'I'm sorry, Madam.'

'What do you *do* with your kidneys, Mr Bones?' said little Mrs Simpkins. 'Haven't you a heart?'

'No heart,' said Mr Bones sadly.

Out in the Street, a cold, driving rain was falling. Mrs Whinebite poked her umbrella into my eye and said, 'Do look where you are going, Henrietta.'

'Dear me,' said Lady B. 'What's the matter with everybody this morning?'

I looked at her. Her face under her W.V.S. hat was calm and untroubled. 'Darling Lady B!' I cried. 'You are the only person in the Street today who looks happy!' and I threw my arms round her neck and kissed her.

Mrs Savernack, bowling down the Street at a break-neck speed, caught us behind the knees with her gardening-basket-wheelbarrow, and we both fell to the ground.

The pavement was wet and muddy. I have never seen

Lady B so cross. 'Is it really necessary to wheel that thing about in the Street?' she said, wiping mud off her skirt with her handkerchief.

'Is it necessary to embrace in the middle of the pavement?' said Mrs Savernack. 'It's time Henrietta learnt to control herself.'

'And don't keep nagging at Henrietta,' said Lady B, putting her hat straight, or, rather, at the right angle of crookedness. 'A nice sight I shall look at the Inspection.'

'W.V.S. . . . Bah!' said Mrs Savernack, who is not a member, and trundled away.

When Lady B and I arrived, the hall was nearly full. I, who am what Charles calls the W.V.S. Dog's Body, took a lowly seat at the back, and Lady B, who ought to have sat among the High-Ups, came with me. The hall smelt of wet mackintoshes, and I reflected, not for the first time, that there are more ways than one of wearing a W.V.S. hat.

There are more ways than one of wearing a W.V.S. hat

'I'm not sure I shall stay,' whispered my neighbour on the other side. 'My feet are wet, and I hate to see women throwing their weight about.'

Then there was a stir at the door, and Authority arrived, with Satellites. Authority looked absolutely stunning. I was so overcome that I instinctively rose to my feet, as we used to do at school when the headmistress came in to prayers. Lady B tugged me gently into my seat again.

Authority, who somehow gave the impression that she was enjoying the whole thing, talked for twenty minutes with one eye on the clock. And, as she talked, a strange thing happened. We, the Ordinary Housewives, sat up and began to feel proud. This hasn't happened much during the war. The Ordinary Housewife has gone her dazed way, being told to eat more of This and less of That, and then, almost directly afterwards, less of This and more of That; her proposed Journey, generally the result of a craving to get away from home, has been proved Unnecessary, and abandoned; she has salvaged, patched, bought half-crown Savings Stamps on Monday mornings, and given breakfast-in-bed to her more glamorous sisters home on leave from the Forces. And all the time with the nagging thought at the back of her mind that she was Not Doing Enough. But here was somebody telling her that she was doing quite a lot.

Balm in Gilead! We sat, with our baskets on our laps and our mouths slightly open, and drank it in. 'You women,' said Authority, 'are the Army that Hitler Forgot.'

I gulped. 'Don't cry, you fool,' whispered Lady B, but her own eyes were full of tears.

'Keep it up,' said Authority. 'Go on being steadfast, and patient, and cheerful as you always have been.' There was some uncomfortable shuffling at this, and I felt my own ears go red.

Then out swept Authority and her Satellites, to rush away to the next village with her message of cheer.

'I felt as though I'd been Saved,' said Lady B. 'Any minute I thought I should get up and testify.'

There was a good deal of delay at the door, because everybody waited politely for everybody else to go out first, but we got into the Street at last, and the first person we saw was Mrs Savernack, still trundling.

'I'm sorry I was so rude just now,' said Lady B.

'It was my fault, really,' I said.

Mrs Savernack looked at us in astonishment. 'What *is* the matter with you?' she said.

So we trundled her off with us to have some coffee. While we were waiting I took my W.V.S. badge out of my coat and pinned it in my turban, to wear there as knights of old used to wear their ladies' gloves.

Always your affectionate Childhood's Friend,

HENRIETTA

Y DEAR ROBERT   August 25, 1943

We had a Horse Show in a village near here on August Bank Holiday. Faith, who looks as lovely on a horse as off one, has been invited to ride somebody's hunter, so, of course, the Conductor wanted to go and see her do it, and he and Lady B and Mrs Savernack and Charles and I walked over. It was a long time since any of us had had a country walk, and we all enjoyed it, though our poor feet began to feel the strain before we got there.

The show was in a field near the river, and there was an enormous crowd round the ring and a few thousand bicycles stacked in the hedges. The air smelt of hot grass and horses and leather, and there were a lot of

People in leggings and check caps

people in leggings and check caps, with bits of grass in their mouths. Outside the crowd were the riders, white with excitement, ready mounted, waiting their turn, and under the trees were the patient farm horses, decked out in ribbons and jingling brass. Time slipped backwards with a click, and we were away in the careless and happy days of Peace. Just once an aeroplane passed overhead, and I looked up and said to myself, 'What a target for a tip-and-run raider,' but quickly dismissed the thought from my mind. This rural scene of innocence and charm was not to be marred by thoughts of Hitler.

Charles and Mrs Savernack, who belong to the Horsey World, had tickets which entitled them to sit in deck-chairs, among the High-Ups, with the sun behind them, but though the Conductor and Lady B and I begged them to avail themselves of this grandeur, they insisted upon staying with us among the Ordinary People.

When we arrived, there were a lot of children riding their ponies round and round the ring. Nearly all of them were little girls, sitting easily in their saddles, with their pig-tails flying in the wind. Though outwardly calm in demeanour, it was obvious that they were excited beyond words and would probably be sick in the night.

'Male sex *not* well represented,' said Charles, shaking his head as one little golden-haired boy rode by.

Mrs Savernack snorted. 'Aeroplanes!' she said bitterly.

Then there was a roar from the crowd as a gypsy girl entered the ring on one of the smallest Shetland ponies ever shown. In a cotton frock and a sad absence of knicker, she kept her long, thin legs off the ground with difficulty, and managed to get thrown in front of the deck-chairs.

'I hope she gets a special prize,' said the Conductor in a choked voice. He is always moved by the sight of gallant and unselfconscious youth.

'That's the pony I like best—that pale one,' I said.

'I suppose you mean the dun,' said Mrs Savernack.

'Henrietta chooses horses because they have kind faces,' said Charles.

'That's how I choose people,' said the Conductor.

At the end, the gypsy child—who, to our grief, had not been awarded the prize—put her feet to the ground and the pony walked away from under her.

After that it was the jumping, which was much the same as it always is in a Horse Show: the horses showing an intense reluctance to jump at all, and rather more determination than usual about refusing at the brick wall. The people in the crowd, who knew nothing whatever about it, gave a lot of advice and shouted 'Whoops!' at every jump, which made the horses even more disinclined to jump than they had been before. One lady, dressed as for Ascot—in a black silk frock and long ear-rings—gave so much incorrect information in a loud voice that Charles became fascinated, and turned his back on the ring in order not to miss a word.

'It's hard to believe,' he said in an awed whisper, 'that *anybody* could know so little about anything and say so much.'

'You find the same things at concerts,' said the Conductor. 'It's the chap whose favourite tune is "In a Monastery Garden" who shoots his mouth about a Beethoven concerto.'

'And at the Academy,' said Lady B, 'the little man creeping round without a catalogue is the one who knows all about it.'

The Ascot Lady edged a little nearer and gave us a Look. 'I can't think why people who are not interested in Horses come to Horse Shows,' she said. She then proclaimed that the horse which had—wisely, I thought—refused the five-barred gate hadn't had a chance, because the rider had been pulling at the snaffle.

Then it was Faith, and we pushed the Conductor to the front so that he would get a better view. She entered the ring looking superb on a beautiful mount.

'Doesn't she look lovely?' said the Conductor. There were tears in his eyes, and Lady B squeezed his hand.

'I like those light-brown horses. Don't you?' I said.

'Bay,' said Mrs Savernack.

'Bey? Oh, yes, bay, of course.'

Faith trotted with the others round the ring in a demure procession. As she passed our corner, she gave us a dazzling smile, and there was a burst of applause from the crowd.

'Her hands are all wrong,' said the Ascot Lady, and the Conductor turned and glared at her through his spectacles.

'Keep your chin in, Faith darling,' said Charles in a low voice.

Faith kept her chin in, and a little smile at the corners of her mouth. When they began to canter, her light-brown horse—whose name was Alexander, and who was obviously enjoying every minute of his appearance in the ring—neighed loudly and began going sideways, like a crab.

'She'll fall off!' cried the Conductor.

'Nonsense!' said Charles.

In the end, Faith and Alexander won the first prize, and Faith cantered away with a card and a blue rosette between her teeth.

'Who said her hands were wrong?' said the Conductor, turning round, but the Ascot Lady had disappeared.

The next thing that happened was that the dun I had picked out got a medal for being the best pony in the show, so you see, Robert, there is something in a kind face, after all.

We got terribly tired walking home.

Always your affectionate Childhood's Friend,

HENRIETTA

83

M<small>Y</small> D<small>EAR</small> R<small>OBERT</small>
　　The Linnet has passed her finals and is now a State Registered Nurse. When she was a small, pink baby, lying in her cradle, I used, as mothers will, to plan careers for her. Anything from a ballet dancer to a Member of Parliament seemed possible and even probable, but I never thought of a State Registered Nurse. Which just shows Fate always has a surprise up her sleeve for you. The Linnet says she never thought of a State Registered Nurse either; the war thought of it for her.

The Linnet was so gloomy about her chances, and told Charles of so many frightful mistakes she had made in her exam, that we began to be quite anxious about the result, and it was a great relief to us both when she rang up, stammering and choking with excitement, to say she had passed.

'I feel like Christian when the load fell off his back!' she shouted.

'I'm sure you do, darling,' I said, holding the receiver a little further away from my ear.

This was obviously an occasion for celebrating, and leaving undone a great deal I ought to have done, I mounted the bus and the Linnet met me in our Cathedral City with a beaming smile. We went off and had the biggest tea that Lord Woolton allowed us. 'I feel just as though I were taking you out at Half Term, Linnet,' I said. 'It is almost impossible to realise that you are a married woman.'★

The Linnet arose from her chair with a shriek. 'I've forgotten to send Philip a cable to say I've passed!' she cried, and rushed from the Olde Tea Shoppe.

★It must sometimes have been difficult for Linnet to realise that she was now a married woman and had been for several months by this time. Philip had been posted overseas and she continued living in the Nurses' Home.

She came back later a little subdued, having failed to send her cable. Apparently, if you are in one sort of army in the Middle East you can have cables sent to you, but if you are in another you can't. It all seemed rather confusing, but nothing daunted the Linnet for long that afternoon, and she dragged me off to the hospital to see her new uniform.

I was relieved to find that in spite of State Registration there was a familiar disorder about the Linnet's bedroom. The new uniform was blue, and brought out the colour of her eyes. It was nice, but I must say I shall be glad when there is plenty of starch and nurses can go back to their white aprons again. The Linnet took a neat little white bow and put it under her chin and pinned the strings on the top of her head. I watched, entranced. Then she took a square of white cambric, put it on the floor, folded it this way and that, and put it also upon her head, and fastened it at the sides with kirby-grips.

'How's that?' she said.

I looked at my daughter. Her eyelashes seemed even longer than usual, little tendrils of hair curled up over the edge of her cap, and the bow under her chin gave a piquant, and at the same time touching, effect.

'I think you look sweet, Linnet.'

'Then why are you crying, you silly little thing?' said the Linnet, sitting down beside me on her bed.

'It's all turned out so different from what we'd planned for you,' I said, and a tear dripped off the end of my nose. 'We meant you to go to Paris, and then be Presented, and then go and stay with Uncle James, and here you are a State Registered Nurse.'

'It's not such a bad thing to be—a State Registered Nurse,' said the Linnet, stroking my hand.

'It's a *wonderful* thing to be, Linnet. That's why I'm crying.'

'You are funny,' said the Linnet. 'Now come and see Ivan Trickey.'

The Babies' Ward was open to the sky all down one side, and the afternoon sun lay in a golden bar across the floor. Several small children who were out of bed began shouting, 'Nurse Linnet! Nurse Linnet!', and ran and clasped her round the knees. A very young nurse who, with limpid brown eyes above her mask, looked as seductive as any Eastern lady in a yashmak, was bathing a very small baby in a basin. The baby was yelling and showing toothless gums.

'Isn't she adorable?' said the little nurse.

'She doesn't seem very ill, does she?'

'She was. She's going out tomorrow, worse luck,' said the little nurse with a sigh.

The Linnet led me round the ward. Some of the children were playing happily, but some of them lay very quietly in their cots—too quietly, and I reflected, not for the first time, that sick children and cats with mice were two of the Almighty's inscrutable ways which took a bit of explaining.

Bathing a very small baby in a basin

'There's Ivan Trickey,' said the Linnet proudly.

Ivan Trickey was sitting up in his cot. His face was covered with a white lotion and his head was shaved. What hair he had appeared to be pale pink, and his arms were in splints to stop him scratching.

'I love him so much,' said the Linnet in a strangled voice, 'that I'd like to adopt him.'

'Darling,' I said, 'if you're really going to have four of your own, do you think it would be wise? I mean, school bills and all that. Besides, his mother probably loves him.'

'She'd be mad if she didn't,' said the Linnet.

Ivan Trickey gave me a long, searching look, then laid his head on his knees and wept as though his heart were breaking.

I was horrified, but the Linnet said, 'He only wants his supper. He's terribly greedy.'

In the last bed was a child twitching and snoring, its head on a mackintosh sheet. The Linnet said it looked like a head injury and must have been admitted while she was off duty. Outside in the corridor was the mother, crying. I wanted to take her hand and say, 'Don't worry. This is a lovely ward, and they'll do all they can for your baby. The nurses are kind. This one with the curly hair is my daughter, and she loves children. She was a child herself only a short time ago.' I wanted to say it more than anything else in the world, Robert, but could I? No. My tongue clove (or is it cleaved?) to the roof of my mouth and I stood there goggling till the Linnet led me away, and now I have another Grinding Regret to chew over when I wake in the night.

When I got home I found Charles deeply gratified by a letter from Bill's Colonel. 'The boy's not doing at all badly,' he said, handing me the letter.

It was a lovely letter and I glowed with pride as I read it. 'Haven't we got nice children, Charles?' I said.

I wanted him to say, 'Yes, darling. It's because you brought them up so beautifully.' But all he said was, 'Some people strike lucky with their children and some don't.'

Always your affectionate Childhood's Friend,

HENRIETTA

M Y DEAR ROBERT   September 22, 1943

Since last I wrote, we have had a Dogs' Jamboree
here in aid of the Red Cross. For a week before I spent all
my spare time brushing Perry and polishing him with a
velvet pad, and I must say that on the day of the show, with
his yellow collar and lead, he looked very fine indeed.

Lady B was waiting for me at the bottom of the hill
with Fay, who was washed and brushed and smelling of
scented soap. She wore a tiny blue bow on the top of her
head. Faith was there, too, for she was on the Committee.
She is often asked to do this kind of thing, because she adds
to the beauty of the scene. The Conductor, among others,
came to look at Faith.

Perry, I was delighted to note, was in one of his
pleasanter moods, neither sulky nor 'Old Dog,' but pranc-
ing along on his neat little feet, and giving Fay some very
meaning looks from time to time out of the corner of his
eye. Perry loves to show off in front of Fay. Nobody quite
knows what Fay's reactions are, as her eyes are hidden
behind her flaxen, spun-silk hair, but Lady B says she is
crazy about him.

It was a lovely autumn afternoon, and the
Savernacks' garden, where the Jamboree was being held,
was full of people. We noticed with pleasure that there
were many side-shows, and a placard at the gate announced
that Madame Zanana would tell fortunes in the summer
house for half-a-crown a time.

Event 1 was the Dog with the Longest Tail (in
relation to its body). This was a dead snip for Perry, who
had entered for this class in several Dog Jamborees, and in
spite of a bald tip, never failed to take first prize. I led him
proudly into the ring, and the first thing he did was to take a
dislike to a harmless and very fat spaniel and set up a fierce
growling.

'Keep that dog in order, please,' said one of the

Judges, whom I at once began to hate as violently as Perry hated the spaniel. Faith said afterwards that our glaring expressions were identical, and she offered, then and there, to give an extra prize for the Dog Most Like Its Owner.

Perry gave a snarling bark and strained at his lead. 'If that dog doesn't behave himself, he'll have to be taken out of the ring,' said the Judge.

'Shut up, Perry, you fool!' I said, and gave him a tiny tap with my finger.

Perry at once became 'Old Dog'. When it was his turn to be judged, he stood on the table trembling all over, and with his nose an inch from the ground.

'It's a shame to bring a poor old dog like that to a show,' said a man in the crowd.

'Perry, *darling!*' I whispered.

But Perry still drooped and kept his tail tightly curled underneath his stomach. Of course, I *could* have pulled it out, but I had a feeling that, if I did, I would be prosecuted by the Society for the Prevention of Cruelty to Animals, so I lifted him off the table and prepared to leave the ring.

As soon as he felt his feet on the ground, Perry forgot to be 'Old Dog', and pranced off with head erect and tail in the air. 'Well, I'm damned,' said the man in the crowd.

The next event was the Dog with the Most Bewitching Eyes. Lady B and I entered Fay and Perry more as a generous gesture towards the Red Cross than anything else, for nobody, except Lady B, who brushes her, has ever seen Fay's eyes, and Perry's expression has never been his strong point. Indeed, he glared at the Judges with such cold dislike that they recoiled from him in horror, and I heard one say that if there was a booby prize for that class he'd know where to give it.

Not even my loyalty to the Red Cross could make me enter Perry for the Dog Most Obedient to its Owner, but he and I found a nice little place in a sunny corner where we could admire Mrs Savernack's word of command and the obedience of her Scottie, who got first prize.

After that it was the Best Groomed, Cared For and Kept Dog. This was the big event of the day as far as Lady B and I were concerned, and we led Fay and Perry into the ring, our hearts thumping with excitement.

There was a big entry for this event, but one by one the owners left the ring until only Fay and Perry were left. When they stood side by side on the Judges' table and licked each other's noses, there was a burst of applause from the crowd.

'These dogs are both personal friends of mine,' said Faith, who felt quite unable to face her responsibilities as a member of the Committee, and she left the ring and went and sat with the Conductor.

'Nice condition,' said the Judge, running his hand down Perry's black satin black. 'What's his age?'

I held up ten fingers and then four.

'Ah, doesn't like it mentioned,' said the Judge in an understanding way, and I wondered how I could ever have disliked him. Then I saw him staring at the bald patch at the tip of Perry's tail, and I knew that all was lost.

Lady B was quite upset about taking the prize from us, but later Perry and I walked away with Faith's Special, 'Dog Most Like Its Owner,' and she felt better about it.

We nearly won the Dog Race (Owner to Run Backwards), too, but just at the finish Perry caught sight of the spaniel and twisted his lead round my legs. Some people fall elegantly and gracefully—I am not one. When I got back to my chair, Lady B said, 'Fancy those knickers lasting all this time. Didn't you get them before the war?'

Faith and I had to wait in a queue until our turn came for Madame Zanana, the fortune-teller. Faith went in first and was closeted with her for a long time. I was just beginning to wonder whether it was worth waiting, even to hear that Bill was going to get a D.S.O., when she came out, her cheeks bright pink and her eyes shining.

'Was she good, Faith?' I said.

'Marvellous!' said Faith, and rushed away. I saw her take the Conductor into a corner of the rockery and kiss him, but there was no time to reflect on this peculiar behaviour, for it was my turn for Madame Zanana, and I knocked at the door and went in.

Madame Zanana was a delightful, apple-cheeked old woman. As soon as I sat down, she said, 'You baint a married woman, be you, my dear?'

Before I had time to reply, there was a knock at the door and Mr Savernack walked in and said, 'What do I owe you, Madame Zanana?', and the Dogs' Jamboree was over, and that was all I got for my half-crown.

But what *do* you think Madame Zanana told Faith?

Always your affectionate Childhood's Friend,

HENRIETTA

Owner to run backwards

November 17, 1943

M Y DEAR ROBERT
Faith is looking radiant. She feels perfectly well, looks lovelier than ever and has produced from her capacious wardrobes some dazzling tea-gowns, which she would never have had a chance of wearing otherwise, and which she changes several times a day. Charles keeps telling her to go for long country walks, but Faith hates walking at the best of times, so she spends most of the day on the sofa, while the Conductor brings her cups of Ovaltine.

Our Faith has always had an eye to the main chance, and she has now started a Sewing Bee for her baby, for which you provide your own materials (bought with your own coupons), and bring your own tea. She was surprised, and rather hurt, when the Baby Bees, as she called them, didn't prove wildly popular, and when people found that they weren't even going to be given drinks before they went home there was a distinct falling-off, until at last the only members left were Lady B, and me and the Conductor, who taught himself to crochet as soon as Faith whispered her secret, and has embarked on a pram rug.

Lady B is a quick and experienced knitter, and has already made one small pink and one small blue woolly coat. She made the pink one first to please the Conductor, who wants a girl, but this threw Faith into such a frenzy that she quickly brought some blue wool and began another. It is nice to know that whichever sex the baby turns out to be, *one* of the parents will be pleased, and, of course, there is just a chance that both of them will be.

Lady B has plumped for a girl, mostly, I think, because she likes knitting pink wool, but she says it is because the mothers of daughters are so much nicer than the mothers of sons, and that Faith has had quite enough spoiling in her life as it is, and it would do her good to have a pretty daughter to throw her into the shade.

She made this announcement during one of the Baby

Bees, and the Conductor was very much upset. 'How can you say such cruel things to darling Faith?' he said, and he threw down his crochet and ran to kneel beside her sofa. 'You ought to remember her Condition.'

'Faith's condition is a perfectly normal one for a young married woman,' said Lady B, crisply, 'and if we've got to tip-toe about the place and talk in whispers for the next two months just because she's going to have a baby, I, personally, shall stay away.'

Lady B says she has noticed a certain amount of War Weariness, anxiety neurosis and Slackening of the War Effort in this place lately, and she has adopted a bracing attitude to counteract it. But nobody is ever offended by what Lady B says to them, and she has certainly done the Conductor, who began the prospective father's anxious pacing as soon as he knew he was going to be one, a power of good.

'Pick up your crochet and go on with it, dear. Darling Lady B is only jealous because she never had any sons

herself,' said Faith placidly, and the Conductor went back to his chair, picked up his crochet, turned in his toes and assumed the heavy frown engendered by this labour of love.

'I suppose I asked for that,' said Lady B, with the greatest good nature.

'I bet Henrietta wants it to be a boy, anyway,' said Faith,

This labour of love

who won't allow us to talk about anything at the Baby Bee except the Bee Baby.

'I don't mind which it is as long as I don't have to push it about in its pram,' I said.

'But Henrietta, I was relying upon you for at least one afternoon a week!'

'Then you're going to be disappointed, Faith,' I said. 'Of all the back-breaking, inside-dropping, dreary occupations, pushing a sleeping baby about the streets in a perambulator heads the list.'

'What a wicked thing to say!'

'I love Bill and the Linnet, and I wouldn't not have had them for anything, but I can honestly say that I have spent the dreariest hours of my life pushing them around in their prams, and I'm never going to do it again if I can help it.'

'But don't you want to push the Linnet's babies about?'

'No!'

'Not even Bill's?'

'No!'

'There's something very hard about Henrietta,' said Faith to Lady B.

'It probably makes her back ache,' said Lady B, who always thinks of something kind to say on my behalf.

'I've been making enquiries about motor-prams, so that darling Faith won't get too tired,' said the Conductor, 'but you can't get them now, because of the petrol. You know, I don't think this crochet is going right. It seems to get smaller and smaller' and he held it up.

'It's a Victory Pram Rug,' said Lady B. 'You'll have to embroider it down the front with three dots and a dash.'

'Three Dots and a Dash,' said Faith dreamily. 'It sounds like Quads.'

The Conductor gave a strangled cry and Lady B patted him on the knee.

'Well,' I said, 'I wish my knitting looked as much like

a baby's bootee as the Conductor's crochet looks like a pram rug.'

Everybody looked at my knitting in silence. It was slightly grey from repeated unravellings, and not in the least like a baby's bootee, or anything else.

'You must persevere,' said Lady B. 'The only thing with that sort of knitting on two needles is to follow the directions blindly. Sometimes it suddenly turns out all right.'

We worked in silence for a little, and then the Conductor went to get Faith's Ovaltine. Lady B and I watched wistfully while she drank it.

'Is it nice, Faith?'

'*Delicious!*'

'She gets extra meat, too,' said the Conductor proudly.

'If anybody gets extra milk, it ought to be Henrietta—she's so thin,' said Lady B.

'Henrietta is one of the people who are not worth preserving in the world today,' said Faith. 'She isn't going to have a Baby, and she isn't doing War Work.'

'She looks after Charles,' said Lady B.

'Lots of us could look after darling Charles,' said Faith. 'He had a hole in his sock yesterday.'

I was just thinking of a stinging retort, when suddenly my knitting came out. 'Look, look!' I cried. 'It *is* a bootee!'

And so it was, Robert.

Always your affectionate Childhood's Friend,

HENRIETTA

95

M Y DEAR ROBERT

Although you are the same age as I am and therefore it is not the slightest use trying to persuade you that I am in my early thirties, I am not going to tell you which week I had to go and register, because I don't see why the Censor, who is no doubt enjoying this letter, should know the horrid truth.

Anyhow, when the Saturday for the forty-you-know-whats arrived, I had to leave my work undone, and a cold lunch for poor Charles, and mount the bus for a Journey to our Cathedral City which was most assuredly not Really Necessary.

'Are you going to Register?' I whispered to Mrs Whinebite, who came and sat beside me.

Mrs Whinebite looked at me with cold dislike.

'I am going to the dentist,' she said. 'I registered *ages* ago.'

'I suppose you're all off to Register?' said little Mrs Simpkins, getting in, rather out of breath, with her shopping basket. 'Ah, me! What a thing it is to be young!'

'Register?' said Mrs Savernack in her loud voice. 'You must be younger than I thought, Henrietta.'

'My dear, I *am* surprised,' said the Admiral, leaning confidentially towards me. 'I had no idea you were so long in the tooth.'

These remarks saddened me, and quite spoilt my ride in the bus, which I usually enjoy.

At the Labour Exchange I was interviewed by a Young Person whose lips were painted where her lips were not.

'Have you any children under fourteen?'

'No.'

'Any help in your house?'

'Part-time help.'

'How many people do you look after?'

'One.'

The Young Person, looking disdainful, wrote down the answers. 'Here's an Idle Creature, I could see her saying to herself, and I had to admit that from the answers I had given there seemed no reason why I shouldn't be whipped into a factory tomorrow. I opened my mouth to explain about Charles, and the secretary, and Matin's departure, and Evensong's chest, and the

I was interviewed by a Young Person

garden, and then I shut it again. There's not to reason why, there's but to make reply at interviews of this kind, and I shall enjoy another ride in the bus, and a jaunt to our Cathedral City to explain these matters later on.

'Your Registration Number?' said the Young Person.

I felt myself getting pink. 'I'm afraid I've done a very silly thing,' I said. 'I've left my identification card at home.'

'Can't you remember the number?'

'No.'

The Young Person gave me a Look. 'What were you before you were a housewife?' she said patiently.

'An artist.' The word echoed sadly round the bare little room, and several of the forty-you-know-whats, who were waiting, leant forward to get a better look.

When I came out Mrs Whinebite was furtively crossing the road to the Labour Exchange. There are times when one simply has to behave like a gentleman, so I stooped down to tie my shoelace, and saw her, out of the corner of my eye, skip nimbly into a tobacconist's a few doors further down.

Coming home, Mrs Savernack sat next to me in the bus. I hadn't forgiven her for her remark on the journey out, so I said, 'I didn't care for that girl's make-up, did you?'

'What girl?' said Mrs Savernack.

'The girl at the Labour Exchange.'

Mrs Savernack is fifty-five and unable to tell a lie. 'I haven't been to the Labour Exchange,' she said crossly. 'I went to try on my new coat.'

After turning round and asking Mrs Whinebite for a detailed account of her experiences at the dentist's, I felt that honour was satisfied, and settled down to enjoy the drive home. But the savour had gone out of it somehow. I felt every day of my forty-you-know-what years. I had rheumatism in my arm, and my face, reflected in the glass of the bus window, looked lined, anxious and thin. When we reached home the bus conductor assisted me onto the pavement as though I were a very, very old lady, and told me to mind the kerb. There was a cold east wind blowing down the Street, and as I hurried along, with shoulders hunched to my ears, I asked myself What I had Done with My Life, and what there was to look forward to but old age, decay and decrepitude.

It was getting dark now, and in spite of the bus conductor's warning, I forgot the kerb and fell down. A passing soldier said, 'Hold up, Mother,' and pulled me to my feet. I thought of my home, dark, cold, with the black-out not done, and the dinner uncooked. I stumbled up the steps and groped my way to the drawing-room door.

Inside it was a blaze of light. A cheerful fire was burning, and beside it sat Lady B with her knitting.

'My dear Henrietta, what is the matter?'

'Oh, Lady B! I feel so old!'

'You mean you feel so cold. Come and sit down by the fire; your face is quite blue.'

'Oh, Lady B! How sweet you are!'

'Nonsense. Evensong's back. She's in the kitchen now, and I'm staying to supper. Why do you feel old? I'm seventy-six and I haven't begun to feel old yet.'

'You never will be old.'

'It's all in the Mind,' said Lady B.

I took off one shoe and held a cold foot to the fire. 'Of course, what makes Registering so awful is that one is simply longing to go off and do something exciting,' I said.

Lady B laid down her knitting. 'I know,' she said. 'I often make up a story in my head that I'm forming a Women's Airborne Army.'

'How lovely!'

'But you ought not to grumble. You are at least looking after Charles. I'm just living in my little flat with my knife, fork and spoon and looking after myself. It makes me feel a very selfish old woman.'

'How can you say that when you've knitted ninety-five jerseys for sailors?'

'But I enjoy doing that,' said Lady B. Then Charles came in. 'Hullo, Charles,' said Lady B. 'Here's Henrietta feeling old.'

'Well, we're all getting up-along,' said Charles. 'But there's still a little gin left in the bottle.'

Always your affectionate Childhood's Friend,

HENRIETTA

M<small>Y</small> D<small>EAR</small> R<small>OBERT</small>   December 15, 1943

We have got a kitten. It is called General James Barton, after Brother James. We had to get it because of the mice, which had taken to scampering over our faces at night, but we felt rather apologetic to Perry, because his breed holds the Ratting Championship of the World, though the gift, somehow, seems to have passed him by. He did catch a mouse once, but only after Charles had hit it with a telephone directory. Perry was frightfully pleased with himself after this, his first kill, and carried the mouse, with low growls, to his basket, where he lay for the rest of the evening with one paw covering the corpse, and his head very erect, like the Monarch of the Glen.

The kitten is an entrancing creature with short grey fur and yellow eyes. When it arrived in its little hamper it began purring before we had got the lid open, and as soon as we lifted it out it made it perfectly plain that it liked us, and was pleased to come and live in our house.

'Isn't it adorable Charles?' I said, as the kitten rubbed its little face against my cheek.

'Not bad,' said Charles, who pretends he doesn't like cats.

The introduction to Perry was a ticklish affair. 'Look, Perry, a darling little kitten!'

Perry looked at the kitten with disgust, and us with reproach.

'Look, General James, a dear little black wog-pog!'

The kitten arched its back and spat, and Perry gave us a Look which said, 'I know I am an Old Dog now, and no use to you, but you might have spared me this insult.' Then he turned, and began walking out of the room.

The kitten scampered after him and caught him up before he reached the door. It ran round in front of him and barred his way. Perry stood rigid, looking over the top of its head. The kitten advanced two steps, and then put out a paw and patted Perry gently on the nose.

Perry looked at us in a bewildered way. 'It's all right, Old Man, it wants to be friends,' said Charles.

Perry looked at the kitten, and the kitten again lifted a paw and laid it, light as a caress, on Perry's cheek. Slowly Perry's long, thin whip-tail began to wag, and Charles and I heaved great sighs of relief.

General James Barton had only been with us a week when he caught his first mouse. It was a very little mouse, hardly old enough to be out alone, but all the same it was a great triumph. He caught it behind the gas-stove while I was putting on the kettle for my hot-water bottle one night. He made a sudden dash, there was some dreadful squeaking, and he emerged with the mouse in his mouth like a sprouting brown moustache.

'Oh, James!' I cried. 'The poor little thing!'

James gave me a malevolent gleam out of his yellow eyes and took the mouse into a corner, where he began doing quite dreadful things. Feeling slightly sick, I went

A malevolent gleam

into the drawing-room, where Charles was reading under his Anglepoise, like a stage star with the floodlights on.

'Charles, the General has caught a mouse.'

'Good,' said Charles.

'But he's behaving in the most horrible way.'

'It is their Nature,' said Charles without looking up. ' "Nature red in tooth and claw," ' he added, with the satisfaction of one who quotes.

'But I really don't feel I can go to bed and leave that torture going on in the kitchen.'

'For the love of Mike!' cried Charles, laying down his paper. 'There are enough awful things going on in the world without getting in a state over a mouse!'

I felt Charles was right, so I went to bed and left General James Barton to his horrid practices.

In the morning he was still playing with his mouse, now, happily, a rather dusty corpse. In the middle of breakfast he began eating it noisily just beside my chair, and its red entrails were spread over the carpet. Even Charles turned a little pale, but he still maintained that Nature Must Have Her Way, and that if we interfered with James's first Kill, he would probably become a mass of repressions and never kill anything else.

Two nights later our Gallant General (now known as Mouser Barton) caught another mouse. But by this time he had become quite blasé about it, and left his prey lying on the kitchen floor. It was while Evensong was away, and when I was getting the breakfast, I trod on it and it exploded with a horrid sound.

When Evensong came back she took a violent liking to the kitten. I encouraged this at first, as she was in low spirits after her illness and needed outside interests.

But she gives him such enormous meals that now he has retired from the mousing business altogether and lies in heavy slumber all night on a cushion on Evensong's chair, and the mice have returned to their carefree scamperings.

Yesterday the kitten insisted upon getting into Perry's basket. This was too much for the old dog, who had been behaving very nicely up till then, and he growled and showed his long, yellow teeth.

'Come along, General James,' I said. 'You mustn't bother old gentlemen,' and I lifted him out.

The kitten immediately got back again. I lifted him out a second time and sat him on my knee. 'If you worry that dog too much he'll bite you, and serve you right,' I said.

The kitten jumped lightly off my knee and got into Perry's basket again, curled up and lay down, rested its little grey head against Perry's black satin side, and immediately fell into an innocent sleep.

Perry looked up at me with a despairing expression, showing the whites of his eyes. I could only shrug my shoulders, for the situation seemed to have got out of hand.

Even Charles lowered *The Times* and looked at Perry in silence. Then he said gravely, 'You know, Perry, even David had a young wife to keep him warm in bed when he was old.'

Perry gave Charles a long, meaning, Man's look. Then he sighed, laid his chin on the kitten's head, and went to sleep.

The kitten stirred and stretched and put one little grey paw round Perry's neck. But Perry never even stirred.

Always your affectionate Childhood's Friend,

HENRIETTA

P.S. When the kitten is not in Perry's basket it sits on Charles's chest. Charles says 'Damn the cat!', but it is easy to see that he is really flattered and pleased. In all the fourteen years we have had him, Perry has never shown him so much kindness.

December 22, 1943

My DEAR ROBERT
As what Mrs Whinebite calls the 'Natal Day' draws nearer, everybody is getting frightfully excited about Faith's baby. The Conductor has lost half-a-stone in weight, and Charles says he is beginning to doubt whether he will pull him through. Faith says she is going to have her

baby on Christmas Day, and as she generally does what she makes up her mind to do, I expect she will. Everybody thinks it is very unreasonable of her to interfere with poor Charles's Christmas, but as Charles and I decided some weeks ago that we would ignore Christmas as much as possible this year, it doesn't really affect us much. What Charles really is worrying about is whether Faith gets him up in the middle of the night or not, and he has promised her half his sweet ration and four clothing coupons if she has her baby between nine thirty a.m. and seven thirty p.m.

The Conductor haunts our house. He is so afraid Charles may go down with flu that he runs in two or three times a day to enquire about his health. As Charles is nearly always out, the Conductor falls to my lot and, fond as I am of him, his doubts, apprehensions and fears are beginning to wear me down.

'She still insists that it's going to be on Christmas Day,' he said this evening, when he arrived and flung himself down into a chair.

'Well Christmas Day is a lovely day to be born on.'

'Is it?' said the Conductor hollowly.

'And if you're worrying about Charles you needn't, because——'

'I'm not worrying about Charles.'

'Oh.'

'And another thing, Henrietta,' said the Conductor, cupping his chin in his hand and looking at me with haggard eyes, 'everybody will expect us to call the baby, Noel.'

'What's the matter with Noel? It's quite a nice name.'

'It's all right, if it *is* Noel, but I am so afraid people will say No-well, like that awful carol.'

Even as he spoke there was a scuffling at the front door, the letter-box was pushed open by cold little fingers, and three shrill, snuffling voices began the well-known tune. 'No-well, No-well,' they sang, beginning flat and going flatter.

The Conductor screamed and covered his ears. I ran out with a sixpence and the carol-singers scampered off into the darkness. I will say that for our carol-singers, they never wait to finish their tune. Give them a copper and they're off in the middle of a line.

When I got back to the drawing-room the Conductor was lying back in his chair, looking white. 'I shouldn't worry if I were you,' I said. 'After all, nobody says No-well Coward. Everybody says Nole Card.'

'No-well . . . No-well'

The Conductor said he didn't like Nole either, but at that moment Charles came in. The Conductor got up at once and went and peered anxiously into his face. 'You all right, Charles?' he said.

'Quite all right, thank you,' said Charles, who is under no delusions about the Conductor's solicitude.

'No aches or pains anywhere?'

'None, thank you; but I want a drink.'

'You look rather grey in the face, Charles.'

'Of course he's grey in the face!' I shouted. 'And so would you be if you had to work as hard as he does. You people have no consideration for anybody. Now go home, and stop bothering him about Faith and her beastly little baby!'

The Conductor turned and looked at me reproachfully. '*Et tu, Brute?*' he said, and walked out of the house.

'Bit hard on the Old Boy, weren't you?' said Charles, as he helped himself to whisky.

'It's all very well, Charles,' I grumbled. 'I have to endure him all day.'

'I sometimes think,' said Charles, 'that Doctors' Wives have a lot to put up with.'

'And it's only taken you twenty-four years to discover! Marvellous!'

Charles laughed and stretched his feet out to the fire. 'You should avoid sarcasm, Henrietta,' he said. 'It doesn't suit you.' Then, after a short silence: 'Do you really hate being a Doctor's Wife?'

'Well, I do rather.'

'Of course, the telephone is maddening.'

'It isn't the telephone so much; though, of course, it does send you crackers sometimes——'

'What, then?'

'Well, I've never yet heard somebody call me the "Doctor's Wife" without wanting to bash them on the head.'

'But you are the Doctor's Wife.'

'I know but people don't say, the "Soldier's Wife," or the "Stockbroker's Wife," or the "Architect's Wife," as though they had no life of their own—at least, only in Germany, which is an uncivilised country.'

'I see what you mean,' said Charles; 'though I can't see why you mind so much. What else?'

'I hate people having to pay you.'

'You'd hate it still more if they didn't.'

'Well, I think it's awful. The other day Mrs Whinebite said: "The Income Tax is bad enough, and now we've got an *enormous* Doctor's Bill to pay," and she glared at me.'

'You needn't worry,' said Charles. 'She hasn't paid it.'

'And then people seem to think that because I'm a Doctor's Wife I ought to know all about illness. The other day, down at the Bee, they were all talking about a new drug called Pentsimon.'

'That's a flower, but let it pass.'

'And when I said "What is Pentsimon?"——'

'The word is "Penicillin" actually.'

'——they all said, "Fancy the Doctor's Wife not knowing!" and there were peals of merry laughter, and somebody said, "Poor Charles." '

'What you want is a little gin,' said Charles.

'There isn't any.'

'Oh, yes there is. I put away a little drop for the day when I might come home and find you very, very low. And I think, my dear Henrietta, that day has arrived.'

Always your affectionate Childhood's Friend,

HENRIETTA

January 12, 1944

MY DEAR ROBERT

Faith always said she was going to have her baby on Christmas Day, and she did. The birth was what the doctors call 'easy and uneventual' (as though any birth could be either!), and Faith came through with flying colours, but we had a terrible time with the Conductor.

It was about four o'clock on Christmas Eve morning when I woke up and found the Conductor sitting on my bed.

'It's me,' he said, in a shaking voice. 'Faith's begun.'

'Did the nurse send you?' Charles opened one eye to ask the question.

'Nurse doesn't know yet. I thought I'd better come for you first. Darling Faith woke up and said she felt a distinct Twinge.'

'Go back to bed and don't be a fool,' said Charles crossly. Then he drew the bed clothes up to his chin and closed his eyes.

'Don't worry,' I said, squeezing the Conductor's hand. 'Nurse will send in plenty of time,' and after a bit I persuaded him to go back home to bed.

I was just dropping off to sleep again when the telephone rang. This was the Conductor to say he had found Faith asleep and looking very lovely.

After all these excitements I lay awake until morning and got up feeling cross and tired.

At midday on Christmas Day, Faith really did begin her baby and rang me up to say so. 'Didn't I say it would be Christmas Day?' she said triumphantly.

'Good for you, Faith. No-well.'

'No-well. You'll keep the Conductor with you, won't you? He gets on nurse's nerves.'

'He gets on mine too. You won't let it drag on, will you?'

'Don't you worry,' said Faith, and rang off.

After lunch, just as I was going upstairs to lie down, the Conductor arrived with a note from Charles saying I was not to let him out of my sight until everything was over. The Conductor began his Anxious Father Pacing at once, but after a bit he said he felt stifled in the house, and dragged me out to pace with him in the road outside. It was nearly dark before I could persuade him to come back inside and have a cup of tea. Then, at seven-thirty, when he had worn quite a track on the drawing-room carpet, Charles walked in.

'Is it all over?' croaked the Conductor.

'Good Lord, no. I want a drink, and my dinner.'

'Do you mean to say, you are going to sit here eating and drinking while darling Faith——'

'My dear Chap, I shall look after Faith much better with a hot meal inside me. Now let's all have a drink. Henrietta, you look tired.'

'I am tired, Charles.'

Charles sat down placidly to his dinner, but I could see by the way he ate it, and didn't stop for his coffee, that little No-well must be on the move. The Conductor refused all food and sat glowering at Charles, but later the very strong whisky which Charles had given him, and which he had drunk absent-mindedly, began to work and he dragged me to a chair by the fire, and sat at my feet and began to tell me about the time he had first met Faith, and what she had worn, and what the Conductor had thought, and what he had said, and what she had said. The fire was warm, the Conductor's voice is soothing, and my head began to nod. When Charles came in later the Conductor and I were both asleep.

The Conductor and I were both asleep

'Morning, Daddy!' said Charles brightly.

The Conductor sat up and blinked like an owl. Then he turned pale-green. 'Charles——' he faltered.

'It's all right,' said Charles. 'You've got a daughter. Faith's fine.'

The Conductor sprang to his feet with a yell. 'I've got a daughter!' he shouted, and began capering around the room. 'Wake up, Henrietta, I've got a daughter!'

'No-well, No-well,' I said flatly.

'Are you absolutely exhausted, Henrietta?' said Charles kindly.

'Absolutely, Charles. Was the baby born on Christmas Day?'

'Five minutes to spare.'

The Conductor capered into the hall, and back again with his hat and coat. 'Is darling Faith disappointed because it's not a boy?' he said.

'Not a bit. She says she's going to have a boy next year.'

'God forbid,' I said, and went out to the kitchen to fill my hot-water bottle.

Always your affectionate Childhood's Friend,

HENRIETTA

M^Y DEAR ROBERT   February 23, 1944
I have been to a party, or rather a partee, because it was given by Americans.★ When George, who is a very old friend as well as being an American, rang up from our Cathedral City and asked me to the partee, Charles, and Lady B, and Faith, and the Conductor thought he was trying to be funny.

I returned to the telephone. 'Are you being funny, George?' I said.

★The south-west of England was by now full of friendly American troops practising for the invasion of Europe. Linnet remembers seeing General Eisenhower in Exeter.

'Funny? Hell! I'm assking you to a partee. I thought you said you liked partees?'

'I do like parties, and I think it's very sweet of you to ask me.'

'I like arsking you,' said George in an exaggerated English voice. 'As a matter of fact, it's a wedding.'

I put down the receiver and returned to the drawing-room. 'It's a wedding,' I said.

'I suppose the poor girl hasn't got a mother

'Are you being funny, George?'

and they want somebody to tell her the Facts of Life,' said Charles.

'She probably has got a mother,' said Faith, 'and they want another middle-aged woman to keep her company.'

'Perhaps George just wants Henrietta to go with him,' said Lady B kindly.

'But Henrietta never *goes* to parties,' said Faith.

'Nor will you, Faith,' I said, 'when little No-well is grown up.'

'I will!' said Faith.

'Well, she won't like it. Girls like their mothers to sit at home with their knitting.'

'You go and enjoy yourself,' said Charles.

I went back to the telephone in the hall. 'Hullo?'

'Hello, I thought you'd gone for one of those long country walks you English are so keen about.'

'I'd love to come to the partee, George.'

'Fine.'

I returned to the drawing-room and found everybody discussing my clothes. 'She hasn't a thing fit to wear,' said Faith.

'There's my Fuchsia,' I said.

'With three darns down the front of the skirt,' said Faith witheringly.

'If you're going to this thing at all,' said Charles, 'you must go properly dressed.'

'You must get a new frock,' said Lady B firmly. 'You don't want the Linnet to be ashamed of you.'

'And do make up your face properly, Henrietta,' said Faith. 'Don't just dab some powder on your nose and think that's enough.'

In the end, I bought a new frock, *and* a new hat, and the Squander Bug sat on my pillow all night, singing in a high, thin little voice.

On the morning of the party, Charles sat up in bed and said: 'How's the Party Girl?'

'I'm not going,' I said. 'It's a very cold day, I feel tired and I know I won't enjoy myself.'

'You must go,' said Charles, 'if it's only to amuse Lady B and me. Besides, you promised. You don't want George to go back to America and say English women don't know how to behave, do you?' So I went.

I arrived in our Cathedral City cold and low in spirits. In spite of a careful make-up, my face, in the glass of the hotel Ladies' Cloak, looked pink in some places and blue in others. The Linnet and George were very kind to me all through lunch, and told me how much they liked my hat and my frock, but my thoughts kept turning in a nostalgic way to my home, and Charles, and Perry, and Evensong, and the kitten, and I wondered how they were getting on without me. Then we got into a taxi and went to the wedding.

Towards the end of the service George bent down

and whispered: 'Cheer up. You'll enjoy yourself in a minute.' I did.

Outside, in the road, were drawn up twenty Jeeps. The front Jeep had two tin cans attached to it by long strings, and an enormous placard on the back saying, 'Just Married'. Heading the procession was a lorry with the band in it. I noticed that nearly all the officers, who looked like naughty schoolboys, were carrying large, unexploded fireworks.

'There aren't going to be Bangs, are there, George?'

'I'll say there are!' said George.

Then the Married Couple emerged from the church, and the little bride, protesting faintly, was lifted into the first Jeep, the guests and their escorts clambered into the other nineteen, the band struck up a rousing tune, and amid cheers, and a series of shattering explosions, the Procession started.

Our Cathedral City was literally and figuratively shaken. Like a barrage balloon which has escaped from its moorings, my spirits rose and soared. I saw Mrs Whinebite standing in the crowd. 'Hullo, Mrs Whinebite!' I shouted, and she cut me dead.

Outside the station we passed another wedding, all white satin and family veils, coming from the cathedral. They waved to us and we waved to them, and I wondered whether they were enjoying themselves as much as we were.

When we got back to the Mess, the Linnet introduced me all round and everybody began calling me Mummy, which wasn't exactly what I'd hoped for, but half a tumblerful of what looked like orange juice, but tasted a good deal nicer, had induced in me a carefree attitude towards life, and I didn't really mind. And, oh! Robert, how well they danced! I hadn't enjoyed dancing so much since you went away.

'Have another drink, Mummy?'

'Over magnolia blooms and lilied lakes——'

'Why are you saying that?'

'I always say that to see whether I ought to have another drink or not.'

'And ought you?'

'No.'

George and the Linnet, who were listening-in to this conversation, went away to telephone to Charles and tell him I was having a good time.

The one called Big Feet came to see me off at the station, and I kissed him good-bye. I mean, if you've been called Mummy all the afternoon, you can do these things.

Charles and Lady B were at the station this end to meet me. As I got out of the train, Charles said: 'Here comes the Red-Hot Momma.'

Always your affectionate Childhood's Friend,

HENRIETTA

M Y DEAR ROBERT   March 8, 1944
I don't know whether it is the East Wind, or War Weariness, or just that we've taken the slogan 'Is Your Journey Really Necessary?' too literally and not been away from this place enough, but anyhow, everybody has suddenly become very bad-tempered and disagreeable, and if things go on as they are, soon nobody will be on speaking terms with anybody else.

The atmosphere at the Bridge Club, they say, is electric, and the Admiral and Colonel Simpkins are already cutting each other in the Street. Nobody quite knows what their quarrel is about, but the rumour is that Colonel Simpkins left the teapot at the A.R.P. Report Post full of tea-leaves, and the Admiral put the tea-leaves, wrapped in an abusive note, on the pillow of the Report Post bed just before Colonel Simpkins came on duty. Even little Mrs Simpkins, that mildest and sweetest of women, had a flaming row with Mrs Whinebite in the fish shop, and the Conductor and Faith are furious with Mrs Savernack because she says they are spoiling Little No-well. On Sunday the vicar preached a very straight sermon on Charity. The congregation listened in sullen silence, and glared balefully at each other as they shuffled out.

'I'm cross,' said Lady B when I met her in the Street one morning. 'And don't start saying we've a great deal to be thankful for or I shall smack you, Henrietta. I *know* we have a great deal to be thankful for, but I'm still cross. I hate this Street and all the silly people who walk up and down it.'

'This is terrible,' I said, for it is always our dear Lady B who keeps happy and good-tempered, no matter how unpleasant everybody else is.

'Now don't begin saying you don't feel cross too,' said Lady B, glaring at me.

'Well, I'm practically always cross in the Street,' I said, 'especially in an East Wind, but as a matter of fact, I don't feel particularly cross at the moment.'

'Oh, Henrietta, how tiresome of you!'

'I'm sorry, Lady B, but that's the way it is.'

Just then Mr Whinebite passed. 'How's your lumbago?' I said politely. Although Doctors' Wives are supposed to know nothing, I find people get very annoyed if I don't enquire after their diseases.

'Splendid!' said Mr Whinebite. 'I'm getting along like a two-year-old. Small thanks to your husband, though. I've been going to Doctor Rival for a month.' Then he hobbled away. 'You might tell Charles,' he shouted over his shoulder.

'Ungrateful Swine!' I muttered, and then I said it

again louder, and hoped he'd hear.

Lady B grinned. 'Now you *are* cross!' she said.

'Any objection?' I said through clenched teeth.

'None at all,' said Lady B in a strained voice.

For the first time in our lives we looked at each other with cold dislike, and then the Siren went. Everybody said, 'There's the Siren,' and looked up at the sky, and cocked an ear at a faint humming which was coming from the sea.

'I do *hate* the Siren,' said little Mrs Simpkins, coming out of the butcher's, 'and we live so far away.'

'Come home with me,' said Mrs Whinebite, 'and we'll have a cup of tea,' and she tucked her hand under little Mrs Simpkins's arm and led her away.

The humming grew louder and there was some gun-fire along the coast. 'I wouldn't stand about in the Street, if I were you,' said the Admiral, who had appeared from nowhere in a tin hat.

Lady B and I betook ourselves to the porch of the bank, and Lady B said that if the bank received a direct hit we might, in death, be surrounded with wealth as we never had been in life.

' "Received" is an awful word,' I said. 'Why do things always receive direct hits instead of getting them?'

'It's a good-enough word for a bomb,' said Lady B.

Pop-pop-pop-pop-pop.

'Damn the Germans,' I said.

Crump, crump.

'Damn the bloody Germans!' said Lady B.

Mr Whinebite came hobbling up the Street and paused outside the bank, 'You know, Henrietta,' he said earnestly, 'it was only because Charles was so frightfully busy. He always said it would be a long job, and——'

'If you're going to talk about your lumbago, you'd better come in here,' said Lady B. 'Remember, everything that Goes Up has got to Come Down.'

116

Mr Whinebite joined us in the porch and went on talking about his lumbago. There were a few more Bangs and then an aeroplane flew out to sea. A minute later a Spitfire streaked across the sky in pursuit and everybody began cheering.

'Atta Boy!' shouted Mr Whinebite, and executed a caper on the pavement, in the middle of which he uttered a loud shriek and clapped his hand to his back. I opened my mouth to say 'I thought you said your lumbago was cured,' but thought better of it.

Soon after that the All Clear sounded and Lady B and I went off to have some coffee. A little farther up the Street we saw the Admiral and Colonel Simpkins going into the pub together, arm-in-arm, their tin hats on the backs of their heads.

'Isn't it *awful*,' said Lady B, 'that we have to have a German plane over us to stop us being disagreeable and make us realise that we have a Great Deal to Be Thankful For?'

'It may be the East Wind,' I said.

'That's no excuse,' said Lady B. 'We ought to be extra happy and extra kind so that we can help the people who have really got something to be miserable about, and all we do is to Bite, Scratch, and Sting.'

'You've said it, Boss.'

'Just because you've been to an American partee, Henrietta, there is no reason why you should cease to speak in your native tongue. But, as I was saying, we've got to mend our ways, East Wind or no. Do you remember the poem by Robert Louis Stevenson?

"I have faltered more or less
In my great task of happiness——
Te-tum te-tum te-tum te-tum,
Te-tum te-tum te-tum te-tum,

Te-tum te-tum te-tum te-tum,
Te-tum te-tum te-tum te-tum,
Lord, thy most pointed pleasure take
And *stab* my spirit broad awake." '

Lady B picked up her coffee spoon

At the word 'stab' Lady B picked up her coffee spoon
and jabbed me in my bad arm.

'All the same,' I said, 'I don't see how you can call a
German plane a pleasure, pointed or otherwise.'

Always your affectionate Childhood's Friend,

HENRIETTA

MY DEAR ROBERT   April 19, 1944
    Doctor Rival, much to everybody's disappoint-
ment, is one of our friends, and he sometimes drops in here
on his way home of an evening. A few nights ago he was
sitting by our fire while he and Charles were engaged upon

one of those sardonic, disillusioned conversations which doctors are so fond of.

'I think,' said Charles, measuring a meagre dose of whisky into his glass, as though it were cough mixture, 'it is time we had a "Salute the Doctor" week.'

'I couldn't agree with you more, Charles,' said Doctor Rival. 'I have felt for some time that the country ought to show us some mark of its esteem and gratitude.'

'Instead of which,' said Charles, 'they are going to take our practices away from us, and keep us so busy filling in forms we shan't have time to look after the sick.'★

'I am seriously thinking of becoming a Quack in the Brave New World,' said Doctor Rival dreamily.

'My dear Rival,' said Charles, 'you have taken the very words from my mouth. I shall have my photo in the local papers with "Cures Guaranteed" written underneath. What line do you propose to adopt?'

'Herbs,' said Doctor Rival simply. 'Practically all my cures will be effected through the post, and I shall sit cosily at home writing my memoirs.'

'It's a funny thing,' said Charles, 'but people really prefer Quacks. I don't mean Osteopaths,' he added hurriedly, for Lady B was rising from her chair in wrath, 'I mean Quacks,' and he got up to see Doctor Rival, who was about to leave, to the front door. 'I sometimes wonder why we waste all those years in hospital.'

'That's the first time I've heard Charles grumble since the war started,' said Lady B, while he was out of the room.

'It's the whisky,' I said. 'He does like a drink at seven and it's running short. But he is tired. I'm trying to keep him in bed for a week-end.'

★A White Paper on the proposed N.H.S. was a matter of fierce debate at this time and Charles was one of 25,000 doctors who had recently received a questionnaire on the subject.

'What's the good of keeping me in bed for a week-end?' said Charles crossly, as he came back into the room. 'If people know I'm there they'll come and drag me out in my pyjamas. Don't be a fool, Henrietta.'

'And that's the first time I've ever heard you speak crossly to Henrietta. You *do* need a holiday,' said Lady B. 'Come and stay the week-end with me. You can say you are going away and nobody need know where you really are. Henrietta can come too, and I'll give you your breakfasts in bed.'

'I think I'd better stay at home and keep people at bay,' I said. 'And, honestly, Lady B, darling, I wouldn't really enjoy myself lying in bed and listening to you rushing up and downstairs with trays.'

And so it was arranged. At first we were pleased and excited about it, but by Friday the impending parting was hanging over us like the Sword of Damocles. I packed Charles's last pair of silk pyjamas and stowed away some neat little parcels of rations. Charles came staggering upstairs under a load of books and tobacco, as though he were about to be marooned on a desert island.

'You know, Henrietta,' he said, sitting down on the edge of his bed and letting the books and tobacco cascade to the floor. 'I feel quite upset about leaving you. Are you sure you'll be all right?'

'Of course I shall. I'll give Evensong the week-end off and have cosy little women's meals on trays.'

'And you'll remember about the clinker in the boiler?'

'I'll remember. Good-bye, Charles; you won't forget me, will you?'

Charles kissed me fiercely, picked up his suitcase, and left the house.

At about eleven o'clock Lady B rang up to say she'd been sitting on Charles's bed and they'd had a lovely talk.

'Did you talk about me?' I said suspiciously.

'We just touched on you,' said Lady B. 'I've given him some hot milk now, and tucked him up for the night.'

The house seemed very quiet and I tiptoed up to bed. The nicest thing about that night was that the telephone rang twice and each time I was able to say, 'I'm sorry, but the Doctor is away,' quite firmly.

The next morning Lady B rang up to say Charles had woken up for early-morning tea

A lovely talk

and a biscuit, but had dropped off again directly afterwards, and she was going to let him bide. At noon she rang up to say he was still sleeping.

'He isn't dead, is he?' I said anxiously.

'Oh, no, Henrietta. He's asleep, and looking so nice.'

'Do you like his pyjamas?'

'They're lovely.'

'You didn't notice the patch, did you? It's on the seat.'

'Well, no. But I'll have a look when he goes to the bathroom.'

The week-end dragged slowly on. Lady B reported at regular intervals. Charles spent the whole of Saturday sleeping, and came down to dinner in his dressing-gown. On Sunday he sat reading in a chair all day. 'He's very quiet,' said Lady B. 'You don't think he's fretting, do you, Henrietta?'

'No, no. Being silent is Charles's way of enjoying himself.'

On Monday I was digging in the garden and looked up and saw an anxious face looking over the wall. 'Charles!' I said.

'I just wanted to ask about the boiler,' said Charles in a hoarse whisper.

'Well, as a matter of fact, it's out.'

Charles gave a strangled cry. 'Oh, Henrietta! How could you?'

'It just went out, Charles. Are you enjoying yourself? You look terribly well.'

'It's heaven!'

'Doctor Brown!' cried a voice from the road. 'Thank goodness you're back! My wife has got the most awful cough. I hardly got a wink of sleep all night. When can you come and see her?'

'I'll come now,' said Charles sadly.

Always your affectionate Childhood's Friend,

HENRIETTA

MY DEAR ROBERT   May 3, 1944
We all feel guilty because Cherbourg has saved us from the Flying Bombs, which is silly, really, because you might just as well feel guilty because you haven't had appendicitis, but there you are. Civilians can never enjoy immunity if they have it. The people who have never heard a siren feel apologetic towards those who have, and those who have been in only a few raids feel apologetic towards those who have been in a lot, and those whose windows have been blown in feel apologetic towards those whose

houses have been knocked down, and so on. Charles says it shows an unhealthy mentality, and the last war taught him to be thankful when nothing was falling on his own head and not to worry about things falling on other people's, but Charles is a mountain of common sense and always has been.

The minor ills which accompany London Raids are now ours. People saying, 'You folk down here don't know there's a war on' is one, and Evacuees is another. Little Mrs Simpkins came round yesterday with a letter from the Billeting Officer saying she had got to have three.

'Three, Henrietta!' she said, handing me the letter, and then she sat down and burst into tears.

I put my arms round her. She felt very frail and small. 'Don't cry,' I said; 'perhaps you'll get a Mother Who'll Help.' This is the forlorn hope of all Hostesses in Reception Areas, but though they sometimes get Mothers, they don't often get Help.

'I'm being very foolish,' said little Mrs Simpkins, wiping her eyes, 'and very wicked, too. We're so lucky down here not having any of these dreadful Flying Bombs, and of course the children must leave London, but I'm getting an old woman, Henrietta, and I find the house without any help all I can manage. I haven't felt very well lately, and I'm so afraid of Breaking Down.'

'You mustn't have them,' I said, kissing her little withered cheek. 'I'll tell Charles.'

'No, Henrietta, no. Please, I really mean it,' said little Mrs Simpkins, sitting up very straight. 'This is Total War,' she said, her eyes flashing, 'and my three Evacuees are one in the eye for Hitler, if you know what I mean, dear.'

'But if you break down it will be one in the eye for Mr Churchill.'

'I shan't break down,' said little Mrs Simpkins firmly.

'I feel much better since I had my little weep, though I **must** say, I hope it never reaches Goebbels's ears.'

'I don't think it will.'

'And it isn't that I'm in the *least* afraid of having a Stroke,' said little Mrs Simpkins, glaring at me; 'but who, I ask you, *who* understands Alexander's stomach as I do?'

'Nobody.'

'I shall manage,' said little Mrs Simpkins, putting a small handkerchief embroidered by Christian Indians in Lahore away in her bag. Then she kissed me, picked up her basket and left the house. I watched her going down the garden path, a small, frail, gallant figure; one of the unsung heroines of the war.

After lunch I went to the Billeting Office myself. Mrs Whinebite was there, having a row with the Billeting Officer. 'It's a scandal!' she shouted as I opened the door.

Having a row with the Billeting Officer

'It's better than Germans in your house, isn't it?' hissed the Billeting Officer. 'It's better than the Gestapo, isn't it? Isn't it better than Rape?'

'*Really!*' said Mrs Whinebite, and flounced out.

'What do *you* want?' said the Billeting Officer crossly.

'An Evacuee.'

The Billeting Officer put on his spectacles and looked at me. 'Well, you can't have one,' he said. 'You're exempt.'

'I know. But I'm stronger than some of the people who've got them.'

'I'm not worrying about you, my dear woman,' said the Billeting Officer. 'It's Charles. I want to keep him fit to look after all these people.'

'I wouldn't let it bother Charles.'

'Well, I'll put your name down,' said the Billeting Officer in a grudging way, rather as though I'd asked for a bit of salmon for the week-end, 'but I can't promise.'

Outside the Billeting Office I ran into Mrs Whinebite. 'Have *you* got any Evacuees?' she said.

'No.'

'Really, Henrietta!' said Mrs Whinebite. 'You ought to be ashamed.'

And so I am, of course.

But I am determined not to end on a Sour Note and also to get this letter to you finished because, at the end of the week, I have got to go into a nursing home and have my arm tweaked, and I shall then be too sorry for myself to pen a line to anybody.★

The worst of going with Charles to see a doctor is that the doctor is always more interested in Charles than he is in me. Once, a long time ago, when Charles used to have time to go about with me, he came with me when I had to have a tooth stopped, and the dentist placed the drill firmly on a nerve in my tooth and then looked over the top of my

---

★Henrietta had 'done something' to her shoulder some time before, attracting varying degrees of sympathy from her friends according to whether or not they suffered from neuritis themselves.

head and began telling Charles a funny story about a mutual patient.

When Charles and I were ushered into the presence of the Great Bone Chief, he and Charles immediately began talking about the Beveridge Report. I sat by the fire and warmed my hands, and began to hope we might get out without my arm being looked at at all, but after a time the Great Bone Chief caught sight of me and said: 'Ah, yes; of course. Take off your jersey, please, and sit here.'

I took off my jersey and sat there.

'If one were perfectly sure the general public would really benefit, it would be simple,' said the Great Bone Chief. 'This arm has only got sixty degrees, Charles. I'd feel happier myself if I thought we'd get the thing working gradually.'

'If we rush it there'll be a muddle.'

'All these meetings—not much rotation here—they don't really get us anywhere.'

'Ow!' I said.

'Of course, nobody has the slightest idea what conditions will be like after the war.'

'Doctors have got enough to do just now, God knows, without going to meetings. I think this needs a bit of help. Shall I come to you?'

'No, no, Old Man, you're too busy. She can come in here for the night.'

At the word 'she' I pricked up my ears, for I felt sure they must be talking about me. 'I'd like to go to the Linnet's hospital,' I said.

This remark was ignored, and the Great Bone Chief went to the telephone and booked me a bed in a nursing home.

Outside, in the street, I said: 'But Charles, I *wanted* to go to the Linnet's hospital.'

'If it's more convenient for him in the nursing home

you must go there,' said Charles. 'Remember, he's a Very Busy Man, and he's Doing You for Nothing Because You Are a Doctor's Wife.'

'Sometimes I wish I wasn't,' I said sadly.

'Weren't,' said Charles.

Always your affectionate Childhood's Friend,

HENRIETTA

May 17, 1944

M<small>Y</small> D<small>EAR</small> R<small>OBERT</small>

Spring is nearly over and Nature's Pride is now a withered daffodil. I don't think the spring has ever been more lovely, and never before has it been so impossible to enjoy it in the simple and uncomplicated way in which the good God intended us to. Lady B says that when she looks at the double cherry-tree in our garden with the blue sky behind it she is filled with an overwhelming sadness. Everybody does everything, whether it is weeding, standing in fish queues, or playing croquet, with a sort of fierce concentration, and tempers are even more frayed than before. Only Little No-well, cooing and chuckling in her pram, her sunburnt face one shade darker than her flaxen hair, and her eyes matching the forget-me-nots in the borders around her, is untouched by the strain and worry of the times.

Since I had my shoulder manipulated I have had to go about with my arm up in the air in a splint. The splint is grappled, as Shakespeare says, with hoops of steel to my bruised and aching body. It looks silly, as well as hurting, is awkward, ungainly, and difficult to negotiate in crowds.

'Henrietta, what *have* you done to yourself?' people

said, surging across the Street towards me, their eyes wide with sympathy.

'I've had my shoulder manipulated.'

'Is that all?' they said, in flat, disappointed voices, as though the whole thing were just a foolish whim on my part.

'Here comes the One-man Band,' said the Conductor. 'You only need a drum on your back, Henrietta, and a Jew's harp strapped to your chin, and a triangle hanging on your splint and you'd be O.K.'

'Take more water with it, my dear,' said the Admiral, with a knowing wink.

Outside the fish shop, squeezing past the queue, I drove the point of my splint into

'Here comes the One-man Band'

Mrs Savernack's ribs. She turned on me, scarlet with anger. 'Is it really necessary that you should walk up and down the Street in that thing, Henrietta, making an exhibition of yourself?'

I put my basket on the ground and advanced towards her with one clenched fist in the air, trying to remember, Robert, what you and my brothers taught me in my childhood about hitting people on the point of the chin, but Lady B stepped out of her place in the queue and led me gently away.

'This is an awful place to live in,' I said in a trembling

voice, after we had sat looking at the sea for some time. '*Awful!*'

'Not awful,' said Lady B. 'Difficult, perhaps, but not awful.'

'Think of London,' I said passionately. 'You only know the people you want to know in London.'

'Pooh!' said Lady B. 'Any fool can live in London, but it's an art to live in a place like this, at peace with your neighbours.'

This had never struck me before, and I turned it over in my mind.

'Living in a small town,' went on Lady B, 'is like living in a large family of rather uncongenial relations. Sometimes it's fun, and sometimes it's perfectly awful, but it's always good for you. People in large towns are like only-children.'

'What a sage you are, darling Lady B,' I said.

'Look at the Big Town people who come to live in the country,' said Lady B, who had evidently given this matter some thought. 'Either they never have anything to do with anybody, which is cheating, because they get all this,' and Lady B waved her hand towards the sparkling sea, 'for nothing, or else they throw themselves into the life of the place and get very angry and upset about things.'

'I got frightfully angry and upset with Mrs Savernack just now,' I said sadly.

'We all have our failures,' said Lady B kindly, 'but on the whole I don't think we do too badly. Even the Londoners settle down after a year or two and begin to take things more calmly.'

'You mean their spirits get broken.'

'If you like to put it that way. But I tell you what, Henrietta,' said Lady B, thumping my knee to drive her meaning home, 'after the war, everybody, even the people in towns, has got to mix up *more*, and *more*, and *more*.'

'More?' I cried dismayed. 'My idea was to go and live in a small flat in London and know five people.'

'You always were a horrid little Isolationist,' said Lady B.

'Yes,' I said meekly.

'Of course, the air raids have mixed the town people up a bit,' said Lady B. 'I mean, you can't rush into your neighbour's house and put out an incendiary in the bedroom and be entirely indifferent to him afterwards.'

'Perfect strangers, they say, make each other cups of tea.'

'There you are!' said Lady B. 'It's splendid. But how are you going to keep that spirit going after the war is over?'

'There will have to be sort of Social Centres in each district,' I said.

'Half the people wouldn't go to them.'

'There'd have to be a law compelling people to go there at least once a week.'

'I hardly feel that would induce a spirit of bonhomie and good cheer,' said Lady B doubtfully, 'and the people who didn't approve of them would say they were hot-beds of gossip.'

'Which they would be, of course.'

'It's all very difficult,' said Lady B with a sigh.

Just then Mrs Savernack came round the corner. She was carrying a heavy basket, which she put on the ground with a sigh before sitting down beside Lady B. 'I'm sorry I said that to you just now, Henrietta,' she said. 'Having had a Bad Arm myself, too.'

'It's all right, Mrs Savernack,' I said, shuffling with my feet.

'I'm so bothered about the boys,' said Mrs Savernack, frowning at the sea. 'It makes me irritable.'

I was torn with remorse. 'And I nearly hit you on the nose,' I said unhappily.

Mrs Savernack stretched out her legs and looked, intently at her large feet. 'I often think,' she said, 'that it would be a good thing if we hit each other from time to time.'

'Gracious!' said Lady B. 'And here have I been advocating Social Centres to promote Good Feeling.'

Always your affectionate Childhood's Friend,

HENRIETTA

June 28, 1944

My Dear Robert

I know you want an ordinary gossipy letter from your home town, but it is difficult to write one this week. We can hear the big naval guns booming away across the Channel, and all our thoughts and our prayers are over there with you all.

On D-night, when the firing began and the planes were roaring overhead, I woke Charles up. 'Charles,' I said, 'it's begun.'

'Nonsense,' said Charles. 'Target practice.'

'It sounds different. And the planes are so low.'

Charles listened, and the old house gave a creak and a shudder. Then he got out of bed and we looked out of the window. The sky was full of coloured lights. Charles sighed. 'Yes,' he said, 'you're right. It has begun.'

'Oh, Charles!'

'Now, don't get in a fuss,' said Charles, clambering back into bed.

'I feel useless.'

'So do I, by God!' said Charles. 'But it can't be helped. We're too old to take an active part in this show, Henrietta, and running round the place with our eyes sticking out isn't going to help anybody. Thank the Lord we've both got plenty of work to do,' and having delivered himself of this sound advice, he pulled the sheet up to his chin and fell asleep.

I lay awake listening to his gentle snores and wishing, not for the first time, that I had the same sane and steady disposition as my husband. The house kept on creaking and shuddering and the planes zoomed over the chimney-pots. I tried not to think of the Linnet's Philip, and you, and the others, and planned a summer holiday in which we were all together and very happy, with the sun shining all the time. 'Escapism,' whispered a voice, so I stopped planning the summer holiday and got up and fetched another eiderdown from the spare room, for the night seemed to have turned suddenly cold.

Lady B rang up in the morning, and said: 'I've dropped two plates and a cup on the kitchen floor already, and I feel there is More to Come. How are you, Henrietta?'

'Cold.'

'Read the first chapter of Joshua,' said Lady B, and rang off.

I read the first chapter of Joshua and felt better for it, then I took my basket and went down the Street.

'The Second Front has begun!' said a lady from the hotel. 'Isn't it lovely? Now the war will soon be over and I'll be able to have my car again!'

The Street seemed to be full of young wives with white, set faces, pushing perambulators. I longed to say something to them, but was afraid to. I still seemed very cold.

The Linnet came home to supper and sat on my knee. This always distresses me, for it means she is unhappy. It also deprives me of the use of my legs for several hours afterwards. Charles came home steady and sane. He said to the Linnet, 'Your mother keeps wrapping herself in a rug and looking like a sick monkey.' This made us all laugh and we had a drink and felt better. Lady B rang up after supper and said: 'Read the last bit of the Epistle of Paul to the Ephesians.' The Linnet and I read it together and she said: 'It steadies you, doesn't it?' and I said, 'Yes.' Then I went to see her off on the bus. As she was getting on, she turned round and said: 'Put on some more woollies, Mummy.' Her face looked very white as the bus turned the corner, and reminded me of the days when I used to see her off on the school train.

The next morning, determined not to be a sick monkey any more, I put on all my winter clothes and went down the hill whistling the waltz out of the Nutcracker Suite.

The first person I met was Mrs Whinebite. 'Henrietta!' she said in a shocked voice, 'just fancy whistling at a Time Like This!'

'I——'

Mrs Whinebite looked at me coldly. 'Of course, your son is in Palestine,' she said, 'but you might have a little consideration for the Feelings of Others.'

'I'm sorry,' I said, and crept away feeling ashamed.

As I turned the corner, I ran straight into the Admiral. 'God bless my soul!' he said. 'What a long face!'

I smiled weakly.

'You mustn't go about looking like that at a Time Like This, Henrietta,' he said. 'Think how depressing it is for other people.'

Tomorrow, I think, I shall do the shopping in my gas-mask.

George, our American friend, arrived here a week or two ago in a Jeep, and with quantities of luggage.

'My, dear George,' I said, running out into the yard, 'have you come to live with us?'

'No, I've come to say good-bye. I was wondering

whether you and Charles would mind very much if we parked a few things in your attic. It's Boots mostly.'

'My dear George,' I said, 'we would be proud,' and I meant it, for George's Regiment was once Cavalry, and when their horses were finally reft from them they clung sadly to their Boots, even bringing them across the Atlantic with them, and taking them out and singing to them from time to time.

I took George and the suit-cases up to the attic, which Charles and I have emptied three times because of incendiary bombs, but which always seems to fill up again almost immediately.

'You see?' said George, unlocking one of the suit-cases and taking out a Boot.

'Beautiful,' I said reverently, for Charles has taught

'Beautiful,' I said

me to appreciate a good riding boot when I see one. 'You don't want them rubbed with banana skins or anything, do you?'

'No, no. Just leave them in their cases. This pair belongs to Big Feet.'

'I shall be able to creep inside if we have bad air raids.'

But George wasn't laughing at my jokes that day. He stood up. 'Good-bye, Henrietta,' he said. 'You, and Charles and the Linnet——' He made a vague gesture with his hands. 'I shall treasure the memory of your friendship till I die.'

'Oh, George!'

We walked downstairs hand-in-hand. In the hall I kissed him and said 'God bless you.' George said, 'I'll write to you from Paris.' Then he said, 'Whoo-hoo,' and waggled his behind as he walked up the steps to the yard.

Always your affectionate Childhood's Friend,

HENRIETTA

August 9, 1944

My DEAR ROBERT
We have been having a terribly anxious time with little Mrs Simpkins, who fell downstairs and broke her leg. It all happened last Wednesday evening when she took one of her Evacuees, who had a cold, some blackcurrant tea to drink in bed. Colonel Simpkins was sitting downstairs reading *The Times*, and he suddenly heard the most awful thumping and bumping, and when he rushed out into the hall there was little Mrs Simpkins at the bottom of the stairs in what novelists call a Crumpled Heap.

Mrs Simpkins fell downstairs

When Charles and I arrived, she was sitting up looking white, and with one of her feet pointing at a very peculiar angle indeed. Colonel Simpkins, like all husbands who love their wives and are anxious about them, was being cross.

'Why didn't you put on the *light*, my dear Emily?' he was saying in an exasperated way as Charles knelt down beside her and put a finger on her pulse.

'I'm perfectly all right, Charles dear,' she said, closing her eyes. 'If somebody would just open a window somewhere——'

'Got any brandy Colonel?' said Charles.

'I never touch it,' said little Mrs Simpkins weakly, resting her head on Charles's shoulder.

'I know you don't,' said Charles in his soothing way, 'but this is Medicine.' He gave me a Look and I went upstairs. I had a feeling that Mrs Simpkins was the sort of person who would have a medicine glass in a small cupboard in her bedroom, along with the tablets, the liniment and the lozenges. I was right.

Brandy proffered in a medicine glass is a very different thing from brandy in a wine glass, and little Mrs Simpkins sipped it gratefully while Charles went out to his car to fetch some splints.

When he came back she was sitting up, looking a good deal pinker. 'That's right, Charles, dear,' she said. 'Just put one of those things on and then you and Alexander must help me upstairs.'

'You're for the hospital, my dear,' said Charles.

Little Mrs Simpkins opened wide china-blue eyes. '*Hospital?*' she said. 'Don't be ridiculous, Charles. Who's going to look after Alexander?'

'I can look after myself perfectly well, thank you, my dear Emily,' said Colonel Simpkins testily.

'You can't,' said little Mrs Simpkins, glaring at him.

'He can look after himself better if he hasn't got to keep rushing up and down stairs with trays for you,' I said.

'And Mrs Whinebite can have the Evacuees,' said Charles.

'Oh, dear,' said little Mrs Simpkins, her lip trembling. Then Charles and Colonel Simpkins carried her out to the car and she was driven away, and I went upstairs to pack some of her old-world nighties into a suit-case.

It turned out to be a bad break, and little Mrs Simpkins had to be under an anaesthetic for quite a long time before the Great Bone Chief from our Cathedral City got it straight. She stood the operation splendidly and was as brave as a lion, and then, three days afterwards, she suddenly gave up trying and turned her face to the wall. 'I'm tired,' she said. 'The war has gone on too long.'

'Goodness!' said Charles, 'you mustn't give in now the end is in sight.'

But little Mrs Simpkins kept on saying, 'I'm tired,' and Charles began to look grave.

Colonel Simpkins was beside himself with grief and anxiety. He kept on coming into our house and puffing out his cheeks in a distraught way, and saying: 'I blame myself; I should have done more to help her.'

Three days of this began to get me down. 'Now, look here,' I said, 'it's silly to talk like that. You know perfectly well you are the Model Husband. Only last week Mr Savernack said he was sick of having you held up to him as an example because you dust the drawing-room as well as doing the boiler.'

This pleased Colonel Simpkins, but he soon began to puff out his cheeks and look miserable again, and in the end I promised I would go and see little Mrs Simpkins and point out to her that she was behaving selfishly.

When I arrived at the hospital she was lying with her eyes shut looking very frail. 'How are you, darling?' I said.

'Tired,' said little Mrs Simpkins, without opening her eyes. 'Tired.'

'You *are* trying your hardest to get better, aren't you?'

'No,' said little Mrs Simpkins.

'But think of poor Colonel Simpkins.'

'Alexander is a most fascinating man,' said little Mrs Simpkins. She then mentioned the names of several elderly spinsters and widows, any of whom she considered would make Colonel Simpkins a satisfactory second wife.

'But if you die you may find that you have to work just as hard in the next world.'

'Oh no, dear,' said little Mrs Simpkins. 'The Lord wouldn't do a thing like that. Not to an old woman who's had Evacuees.'

This defeated me and I sat in silence for several minutes. Then I said: 'They've been trying to blow up Hitler.'

Mrs Simpkins opened her eyes for the first time. 'Who has?' she said.

'The German Generals.'

'It was a failure?'

'Yes. But they blew his trousers off and singed his back hair.'

Little Mrs Simpkins began to laugh weakly. 'Really!' she said. 'How very humorous! His trousers! Dear me!'

'People seem to think there will soon be civil war in Germany.'

'Why didn't you tell me this before, Henrietta?' said little Mrs Simpkins, sitting up in bed.

'Everybody is frightfully pleased and excited, except poor Colonel Simpkins, who keeps on worrying and worrying about you all the time.'

'He needn't worry any more,' said little Mrs Simpkins, 'I'm going to get better. Back hair, indeed! I haven't been so amused for a long time.'

Always your affectionate Childhood's Friend,

HENRIETTA

September 6, 1944

My Dear Robert
    I met Lady B on the cliff path a few days ago. She was carrying a basket which was much too heavy for her and puffing slightly. I took the basket from her and led her to a seat. She sat there in silence for a few minutes, breathing deeply, then she said, 'Henrietta, I am a wicked woman.'

'Good gracious, Lady B, darling!' I said. 'What have you been doing?'

'It isn't doing, it's thinking,' said Lady B darkly.

'What have you been thinking?' I said with deep interest, for Lady B's thoughts are always piquant and sometimes surprising.

'Here we are with all this beauty——' she waved her hand at the sparkling sea, 'no sirens, no tip-and-runs—days of sunshine and nights without fear——' She paused.

'Well?'

'And when people from London tell me Flying Bomb Stories I want to bang them on the head.'

'That's nothing,' I said, 'I've wanted to do that for some time.'

'It's jealousy, of course,' said Lady B, 'because we can't tell Flying Bomb Stories ourselves which show us up in a good light.'

'And partly because we're in a hurry. It took me three-quarters of an hour to get up the Street yesterday to buy a stamp.'

'I'm thinking of having a little placard pinned to my bosom, saying, "I think you were SIMPLY WONDERFUL." '

'I don't mind the "My dear, I ran screaming into the Tube" ones a bit. Do you?'

'Not a bit. It's the ones that end, "Of course, I never moved from my desk; somebody must Set an Example" that get me down. I always feel so terribly sorry for the other people in the room who get under the table.'

'And, of course, they are just a wee bit cross with us for not having the Flying Bombs here.'

'It's perfectly natural. I should be exactly the same myself. But I tell you what, Henrietta,' said Lady B, prodding my knee with her forefinger and gazing earnestly into my face, 'I think we British, as a nation, will have to go easy on Bomb Stories to the Americans after the war, or they'll all hate us.'

'You're dead right.'

'It's a pity,' said Lady B, with a sigh. 'I was looking forward to getting hold of an American woman and telling her about the time the bomb hit our church.'

'And how you went on with your lunch and never moved!'

'Exactly!' said Lady B, with a twinkle. 'Well, Henrietta, I must say I feel purged and refreshed by this confession. In future, I am going to look upon Bomb Stories, and being despised and told I don't know there's a war on, and feeling guilty about it, as part of my War Work. I have always said Knitting Is Not Enough, even for an old woman.'

'I used to think that as soon as I'd got Evacuees I'd feel better about everything, but they're so nice I've begun to feel guilty again.'*

'I *am* glad they're nice,' said Lady B. 'How is Charles reacting?'

'Marvellously.'

'Dear Charles!' said Lady B, and then we went home.

I found the Admiral on our doorstep. As soon as I saw his face I knew something must have happened to Teddy, their younger boy, in France. 'We've had bad news, Henrietta,' he said. 'I expect you can guess what it is.'

*A few weeks previously Henrietta had won her battle with the Billeting Officer and been issued with a cheerful family of three.

I nodded and took his hand.

'Alice wanted me to tell you, Charles being his godfather and everything. I think she'd like to see you, if you feel you can face it.'

We found Mrs Admiral frying some fish for lunch. She was quite calm, but her face looked different. I put my arms round her and kissed her, and then took the frying-pan out of her hand. The Admiral looked at us helplessly for a moment and then went out of the room. Mrs Admiral sat down on a kitchen chair and picked up a corner of her apron and examined it closely. 'I keep thinking about him when he was a little boy,' she said in a careful voice.

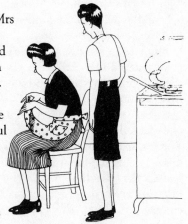

'He was a dear little boy.'

'They both were. It's hard on their father, losing both his splendid sons.'

Picked up a corner of her apron

Then there was a silence. I turned the fish over and there was a great spluttering. 'Hake does spit so,' said Mrs Admiral. Then she said, 'We're not telling anybody, because of the croquet this afternoon.'

'But surely you'll scratch?'

'No, dear. Mrs Whinebite is so very keen, I really couldn't let her down. Besides, I'd like to be occupied. But if people knew about—about Teddy it might make them feel uncomfortable.'

The Lawn Tennis, Croquet and Bowling Club was looking very lovely that afternoon in the August sunshine, and there was quite a little crowd watching Mrs Admiral and Mrs Whinebite playing together in the finals of the Croquet Doubles. I arrived just in time to see Mrs Whinebite make a smashing hit across the whole length of the lawn, and then proceed to go through a lot of hoops.

'Ah—Triple Peel,' I said, as I sat down beside Lady B. I always say 'Triple Peel' when I find myself near a croquet lawn, rather like people who go to Meets on foot and say, 'Not much scent to-day, Master.'

After performing wonders with four croquet balls and fastening several coloured clips to her behind, Mrs Whinebite came and sat beside Lady B and me in a special chair marked PLAYER. 'I'm playing the game of my life,' she said in a low voice, 'and it's just as well, because poor Mrs Admiral can't do a thing.'

Some Visitors from the hotel wandered into the club and paused on the far side of the croquet lawn. Every woman, except Mrs Whinebite's opponent, who had just missed the Stick, immediately lost interest in the game and feasted her eyes hungrily on the Lady Visitor's duck-egg linen suit. 'My dear, *croquet!*' said the Lady Visitor to her companion. Then she gave a little scream. 'Oh! And bowls, too! How sweet! Of course, these people simply don't know there's a war on!'

The Admiral dropped his pipe on the grass. As he stooped to pick it up he laid his hand for a moment on Mrs Admiral's knee.

Always your affectionate Childhood's Friend,

HENRIETTA

M<small>Y</small> D<small>EAR</small> R<small>OBERT</small>   October 4, 1944

Perry is getting very old. His little muzzle is quite grey, and his eyes have a film over them. Charles and I try not to think about him being fourteen, for we love him, although he hardly ever shows us any kindness and becomes more overbearing and masterful every day.

Now that he is old, you'd think that the Walkie question might have become easier; but not at all, dear. Although Perry can no longer go for long walks, his idea is that he should go for a great many short ones instead, and at regular intervals during the day he scrapes the calves of my legs with his sharp little claws as I pass, and looks at me, something near to pleading in his protruding and arrogant brown eyes.

His favourite walk is along the Parade to the barbed wire at the River Mouth, behind which are the notices saying, DANGER. He and I were proceeding in this direction, at a slow pace and with many pauses after tea today, when we met Mrs Savernack. 'That dog's getting old, Henrietta,' she said.

'Only fourteen, Mrs Savernack.'

'That's ninety-eight,' said Mrs Savernack. 'Look at his eyes. You ought to have him put down.'

Perry gave her a look of cold dislike.

'He's perfectly healthy,' I said.

' "Brothers and Sisters, I bid you beware of giving your heart to a dog to tear," ' said Mrs Savernack, with more sympathy than usual.

'I didn't know you read poetry,' I said.

'I don't,' said Mrs Savernack. 'That's the only poem I know, and I don't know all of it, and I don't know who wrote it, but it's got more sense than most.'

Saddened by this conversation, we walked on until Perry met a puppy. The puppy was mongrel, female and would obviously, when grown-up, be no better than she should be. In the meantime she practised her wiles on the old gentleman in black-and-tan. Perry, like most old gentlemen, was flattered by these attentions; his tail began wagging so fast that it became a blur, and he even attempted a little mild frisking.

I was just wishing Mrs Savernack could see him, when the puppy darted roguishly through the barbed wire. Perry followed her, and there they were on the land marked DANGER, surrounded by land-mines. 'Perry!' I shouted. 'Come back at once!'

Perry, not for the first time, ignored my command. The puppy licked his nose and ran round him three times. Perry, a victim to mental and physical giddiness, stood rocking on his feet.

'Come here, you Silly Old Man!' I cried angrily, and began weighing Perry's life and mine in the family balance. The puppy rocketed away still deeper into the danger zone, and Perry followed her, gallantly ignoring his rheumatism.

Perry, not for the first time, ignored my command

I took a deep breath and shut my eyes. When I opened them Dick Sand-Eye was standing beside me. Dick Sand-Eye is an elderly soldier who has permanent and obscure duties in our village, and has endeared himself to the inhabitants by his cheerful demeanour and his rendering of

'Paper Doll' as he goes in and out of a hut which has been built for him just outside the DANGER area at the River Mouth. He is called Dick Sand-Eye because he once got some sand in his eye, and had to go about for several weeks with a pink shade over it.

'If anything happens to me,' I said, clutching Dick Sand-Eye's arm, 'I want you to give my husband my love, and say I have *always* realised that he is too good for me.'

'Now, now, Lady,' said Dick Sand-Eye in a soothing way, 'you mustn't create like that.'

'I'm not creating.'

'Yes, you are,' said Dick Sand-Eye, 'you're leading-off a fair treat. I don't know what the trouble is between you and your husband, but if it's Another Woman, my advice to you is—ignore it.'

'But——'

'There's always a chance of a man coming back, provided his missus doesn't create and lead-off.'

'But——'

'Lots of elderly gentlemen likes a little fling before it's too late, so to speak.'

'Yes, but——'

'But nine times out of ten it doesn't amount to a row of pins.'

'Look here, Dick Sand-Eye——' I said loudly.

'Fancy you calling me that, Mrs Brown!' said Dick Sand-Eye, looking pleased.

'My husband isn't having a love affair with anybody. At least, if he is I haven't noticed.'

'Then why go and drown yourself?'

'I——'

'Drowning's a norrible death. All your past life comes before you, they say.'

'But, look here——'

'Quite apart from the disgrace, and not being buried

sort of book will do. Goodness knows there's enough literary rubbish in your house!'

Saddened by this conversation, I went home to look at my books, and ran my fingers lovingly along their well-worn backs. No, I'd be damned if I'd give away any of my old friends. They might as well ask me to give Perry away to the Red Cross, or even Charles. Then Conscience raised its ugly head. 'No Doodle-Bugs,' it whispered, 'and you can't even spare a book.' I sighed, and went back to the shelves and took one down. *The Princess and Curdie*, only a kids' book, after all, and Bill and the Linnet grown up. But what about grandchildren? 'Not on your life!' I said loudly, and put it back and took down another. *Elegant Woman*—not the sort of book one read, but ah! the delicious illustrations! I put it back. *Brush Up Your French*; that had been on the shelf a good many years, and had I brushed up my French? No. But one never knew. Any moment it might become imperative that my French be brushed up—after the war—*après la guerre*—or was it *le guerre*? I put it back.

But next morning I did manage to wrest a few volumes from the shelves and took them down to the Good Book depot. As I handed them in I felt like a mother delivering her children to an orphanage.

'Is that all?' said Mrs Savernack, in a grudging way.

Books were stacked all over the floor and on the counter. On a shelf in the corner I saw a complete edition of Fielding. I took one down; it was bound in calf, and as I held it in my hand little shivers went up and down my spine. 'What's going to happen to these books?' I asked.

'Pulp,' said Mrs Savernack.

'But it's monstrous! It's frightful! It's a crime!' I cried, getting red in the face. 'Here we are stuck down here: no theatre, no music; the only thing which stops us from becoming screaming savages is books, and now——'

'Pulp, all pulp,' said Mrs Savernack, who dislikes books as some people dislike cats.

'Do go away, Henrietta,' said Mrs Admiral. 'You really are terribly in the way.'

I rushed blindly into the Street, nearly colliding with little Mrs Simpkins in her bath-chair, who was bringing *Stray Thoughts for Girls* as her offering.

On the way home I decided to steal the Fieldings. It was quite simple. That night, while the nine o'clock news deadened the sound of my burglarious entrance, I walked into the Savernacks' house, saw the key of the depot on the hall table, picked it up, and walked out again. Then I went to the depot, lifted the Fieldings tenderly from their shelf, put five one-pound notes on the counter under a copy of *Uncle Tom's Cabin*, returned the key to the Savernacks' hall table, and went home.

'More books?' said Charles, looking up from *The Times*. 'You'll have to get another shelf put up soon.'

Next morning, like a murderer unable to keep away from the scene of his crime, I took another book down to the Good Book depot. The empty space on the shelf where the Fieldings had been yawned accusingly empty, but nobody seemed to have noticed it, and Mrs Savernack accepted *Gone With the Wind* very graciously.

'People are always so wonderfully generous,' said Mrs Admiral. 'Yesterday we had an anonymous gift of five pounds.'

But that evening, just before dinner, while Charles was drinking his whisky-and-soda, Evensong flung open the door and the Police Sergeant and Mrs Savernack walked into the room.

'Hullo, Sergeant,' said Charles, who has professional dealings with the police, 'what's the trouble now?'

The Sergeant scratched his chin and looked uncomfortable. 'Well, Sir——' he said.

'It's Henrietta,' said Mrs Savernack. 'She's stolen some books.'

'I wouldn't put it past her,' said Charles cheerfully.

Mrs Savernack walked across to the bookshelves. 'There they are!' she said dramatically, pointing at the Fieldings.

'I didn't steal them,' I said. 'I left five pounds.'

'What damn-fool nonsense is this, Henrietta?' said Charles.

'They were so beautiful,' I said.

'It was my fault,' said Mrs Savernack, coming to my rescue in a big way. 'I told her they were going to be pulped. Of course, they aren't really.'

'Then I take it you don't want to bring a case?' said the Sergeant.

'Certainly not,' said Mrs Savernack. 'The whole thing was a misunderstanding.'

The Sergeant then refused some beer, winked at me behind Mrs Savernack's back, and left. Mrs Savernack stayed behind to have a drink. She said nobody knew of my lapse—she couldn't call it anything worse than that—except Mrs Admiral and herself, and they would be as silent as the grave. She said she was going to give my five pounds to the Red Cross as a judgment. Then she went away with the Fieldings.

When she had gone, Charles said, 'You silly little thing! I believe you were frightened.'

I said, 'Yes.'

Always your affectionate Childhood's Friend,

HENRIETTA

MY DEAR ROBERT

It is wonderful news that you may be coming home. Do you think we shall recognise each other after all these years, or shall we have to meet under the clock at Waterloo, each wearing a red carnation? Is there still a clock at Waterloo? And are there any red carnations left in London? I wouldn't be knowing. I think we must arrange to meet somewhere else. I suppose some day I shall make a Rip Van Winkle sort of appearance in London again, but not yet. It would be like going to stare at somebody who is very ill and hasn't got her false teeth in—all right for those who are near and dear to her, but an impertinence from strangers.

When I got your letter I sat down in front of my looking-glass and turned it towards the cold light of day. I wanted to take stock of what Charles calls the 'Old Visage', and face up to the ravages of time with what courage I could muster.

The reflection in the glass wasn't frightfully encouraging. Thinner, of course, and the thing in my cheek which used to be a dimple had deceitfully turned itself into a line. Lines, not to say furrows, from nose to chin, lines on the forehead and round the eyes, and a dreadful hint of incipient scrag at the neck. Hair at the sides gone into what I like to call grey wings, and what everybody else calls just grey hair. Eyebrows grown coarse and eyelashes fine. Also a cold.

'What are you doing, Henrietta?' said Charles, coming into my room at that moment.

'I think Queen Elizabeth was right never to look in the glass,' I said gloomily.

Charles bent down and looked over my shoulder at my reflection. 'Worrying about the Old Visage?' he said kindly.

'I'll say I am.'

Charles stared into the glass in silence, then he said, 'Of course, this is a very trying light.'

'Yes, Charles.'

'And you haven't done anything to your face this morning?'

'No, Charles.'

'Personally, I like a woman to have a few lines on her face,' said Charles. 'It shows she uses it.'

'Yes, Charles.'

'Don't sigh like that, Henrietta,' said Charles. 'We can't keep young for ever.'

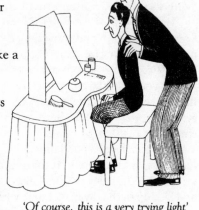

'Of course, this is a very trying light'

'I'm afraid Robert will notice a great change in my appearance,' I said sadly.

'I shouldn't worry about Robert,' said Charles, whom I have never succeeded in making jealous. 'He's probably developed an enormous stomach and a bald head by now. All the same, you'd better go and get yourself done up a bit. I'll speak to Faith about it. It will be good for your morale if nothing else.'

That afternoon Faith came bustling round and found me bedding-out the wallflowers. 'I'm so glad you're going to take an interest in your appearance at last, Henrietta,' she said. 'I've made an appointment for you with my little man on Tuesday. He's marvellous. We'll go in together.'

On Tuesday, Faith and I caught the early train to our Cathedral City. Faith said she had made appointments for everything, and that it would take time. She said she herself would have just a shampoo and set.

Faith's little man, who was called Gaston, looked at

me gloomily when I was paraded before him.

'Madam wishes to change her hair-style,' said Faith.

'That is not the surprise,' said Gaston simply.

'She's going to have a facial as well,' said Faith, 'and a manicure and her eyebrows plucked.'

'Not plucked, Faith,' I said.

'Shaped, then,' said Faith.

'Every small helps,' said Gaston. 'But it is the hair-style which makes the big guns.' He then sat me in a chair, pulled my two faithful hairpins, Castor and Pollux, from my head and threw them carelessly on a shelf. After that he began combing my hair about and twisting my head this way and that, making clucking noises all the time.

'The face is too thin,' said Gaston.

'I'm afraid so,' I said.

'And the brow not sufficiently broad. The eyes also they are too close. It is not in the mode.'

'I'm sorry,' I said.

'We will see,' said Gaston.

Three hours later, when the female assistants had withdrawn with buffers and tweezers, and Gaston was putting the finishing touches to my hair, Faith came into my cubicle. 'Finished?' she said.

Gaston whisked the towel from around my neck. '*Regardez!*' he cried. 'We have here the definite improvement. Yes? No? It is not?'

'My dear Henrietta!' said Faith, in a hushed voice.

I opened my eyes, for I had fallen into an exhausted sleep. A perfectly strange face confronted me in the looking-glass.

'I fill out the hair at the sides to give breadth,' said Gaston.

'Marvellous!' said Faith. 'Don't you like it, Henrietta?'

'I don't think Charles will,' I said.

'Charles will love it,' said Faith firmly.

'I like my finger-nails and my eyebrows,' I said, not wishing to appear ungrateful.

'You look ten years younger,' said Faith. But I didn't. The awful thing was that I looked ten years older. Faith and I went out to have some tea, and every time I saw myself in a shop window my stomach turned over inside me.

When Charles came in that evening I stood up, trembling, but all he said was, 'I've had a terrible day and I'm not done yet.' But half-way through dinner he laid down his knife and fork and said, 'Henrietta, what on earth have you been doing to yourself?'

'It's my new hair-style, Charles,' I said.

'Then I shall grow a beard,' said Charles.

Next morning I managed to coax my hair back into its old ways, but the sad part of the story is that I left Castor and Pollux on Gaston's shelf.

Always your affectionate Childhood's Friend,

HENRIETTA

November 29, 1944

M Y DEAR ROBERT
You remember George, our American, who left his riding boots in our attic and went away to the battle? Well, I got a letter from him a few days ago. It said: 'Dear Henrietta, I have been wounded, getting along fine— Love, George.' The address was a military hospital somewhere in England, and the writing was so shaky that I showed the letter to Charles, who said, 'Hum,' and handed it back again.

'Do you think he's bad, Charles?' I said.

'Can't say,' said Charles. 'Seems a bit shaky.'

'I think I ought to go and see him,' I said.

'Now don't start tearing about all over the country every time you hear somebody's wounded,' said Charles. 'You know we're asked not to travel.'

'Yes, Charles.'

'And Evensong is beginning one of her colds.'

'Yes, Charles.'

'You generally go down with something yourself this time of year.'

'Yes, Charles.'

Then there was silence and Charles went on reading *The Times*, turning over the pages in an angry, rustling sort of way. Then he said: 'If you really feel you must go, you'd better get on with it.'

'Suppose it was Bill, wounded in America, Charles,' I said.

'I know,' said Charles. 'But for God's sake keep warm, Henrietta. There's enough sickness about without having you on my hands all the winter.'

As soon as I decided to go and see George in hospital, I began to be terrified of the journey. I confided my fears to Lady B, who was sympathetic and confessed that the very idea of mounting a train threw her into a frenzy, and considering she had spent the whole of her life travelling all over the world, she couldn't think why this thing had come upon her, unless it was old age.

As soon as it got about that I was going away, everybody came round to give help and advice.

Faith brought a suit-case, which she said held a lot and was light to carry, and little Mrs Simpkins brought a small flask of brandy to go in my handbag.

'I'm told travelling is terrible,' said Mrs Savernack. 'Take care you aren't knocked down and trampled underfoot, Henrietta.'

'If you hear a Flying Bomb coming, throw yourself down, no matter where you are.'

'But suppose it isn't a Flying Bomb?'

'I dare say people will understand when you tell them you come from the West Country and don't know better.'

Next morning Charles took me to the station. On the platform I clung to him as a drowning man to his rescuer. 'If Evensong's cold gets worse, you'll have to go to the hotel for your meals,' I said.

'All right,' said Charles gloomily, 'but who's going to feed the cat?' Then he kissed me hurriedly on the chin and left.

In the train, I remembered I had left my torch behind. The shock was so great I nearly had a swill out of Mrs Simpkins's flask. The train was late arriving at the junction where I had to change, and it was quite dark.

I clung to him

People hurried by, their faces in the dimmed lights looking like the dead; engines screamed, trains shunted, and a Voice of Doom kept booming through a loud-speaker. Everywhere people seemed to be saying good-bye, locked together in desperate embraces.

'This,' I said aloud, 'is what mankind has made of the beautiful world God gave to him.'

'Pardon?' said an old lady standing near.

It was after nine when I arrived at the hospital. 'I know it's long past visiting hours,' I said to the orderly in the hall, 'but my train was very late.'

'Are you Captain Anderson's mother?' said the orderly.

I was surprised at being taken for an American, for Charles always says I am the perfect example of the decayed and disappearing West Country gentry, but then I saw a twinkle in the orderly's eye. 'Temporarily,' I said, and was taken upstairs.

George had cradles all over him to keep the bed clothes from touching him. The lamp beside his bed was shaded so that the light didn't shine on his face, but I could see that he looked very ill. 'Only a minute,' whispered the nurse.

George moved his head from side to side on the pillow and muttered something I couldn't hear. I put my hand on his. 'Hullo, George,' I said softly.

George opened his eyes and looked at me. 'Hullo, Henrietta,' he whispered.

'Hullo, George.'

'Your hands are very cold.'

'Yours are very hot.'

George sighed and shut his eyes. Was it for this that I had flung myself half across England? I shut my eyes, too, and prayed that I might think of just one simple, short, heartening sentence to comfort him in his pain and distress. My mind remained a blank.

Presently he opened his eyes again. 'Hullo, Henrietta,' he said; 'still there?'

'Still here, George.'

'Good,' said George.

'I've got to go now, but I'll come back tomorrow.'

'Good,' said George, and I disentangled my fingers and tip-toed away.

George was better next day, and he went on getting better. I stayed for a week, and before I left I got off some of the things I had thought up in the train, about America, and his mother, and the girl he's going to marry, and he enjoyed them all.

I arrived home with a heavy cold and a temperature and went straight to bed.

When Charles came home in the evening I said to him: 'Every time I shut my eyes I see sort of flashes.'

'What are they like?' said Charles, peering at the thermometer.

'Stars and stripes,' I said.

Always your affectionate Childhood's Friend,

HENRIETTA

MY DEAR ROBERT   January 10, 1945

Charles and I decided that we would have a New Year's party, so we asked Faith and the Conductor to come to dinner. Charles says he enjoys having Faith and the Conductor to dinner, because he and Faith talk about hunting, and the Conductor and I talk about music and poetry and all that, and everybody is satisfied.

Faith and the Conductor were quite overcome when we asked them. They said it was years since they had been out to dinner and that they would hire somebody to sit in their house in case Little No-well should cry.

'Don't be grand,' said Faith, 'it will only make us uncomfortable if we feel we've given Trouble.'

I promised we wouldn't be grand, which was just as well, because the day before the party Evensong went down with her bronchials and left me to cook a chicken.

I am one of those people whose cooking goes to pieces if they are fussed or hurried, so I began preparing the dinner directly after breakfast and sent Charles to the hotel for his lunch. I always hope that when I cook a little dinner for friends I shall be like the Young Wife in the Women's Papers (who is generally alluded to as the Newly-Wed), who has everything ready in good time, and is discovered by her guests in the drawing-room (alluded to as the lounge), wearing a smart gown and with each cocktail glass standing on a dainty doily. But somehow it never works out like that, and when Faith and the Conductor arrived I was making the gravy. Everybody crowded into the kitchen and stood round me, and I lost my head and made Lumps, but Charles brought me a cocktail and I felt better, and then we all went in to dinner, each bearing a dish.

'You look very lovely, Faith,' said Charles, as he always does, and for the first time since I have known her Faith didn't say, 'What, this old rag?' but looked at Charles and said, 'I have brought my apron for the washing-up,' with a sort of limpid simplicity which shook us all.

'This chicken is beautifully cooked,' said the Conductor.

It is for moments such as these that cooks live, so I said I was afraid there might be lumps in the gravy, just to show I wasn't puffed up.

'I *like* lumps in the gravy,' said the Conductor, and from that moment the party went with a bang.

'Do you cook cabbage the way they tell you in *Food Facts?*' said Faith.

'No,' I said. 'Do you?'

'No,' said Faith.

'The great art of washing-up,' said Charles, 'is to have one to wash, one to dry, and one to put things away.'

'I couldn't agree with you more,' said the Conductor. 'Darling Faith gets quite annoyed with me sometimes for not going straight to the scullery with her. She doesn't realise how *very* important it is to get the table absolutely cleared first.'

'A place for everything and everything in its place,' said Charles smugly.

'But it's so lonely splashing about in the sink all by yourself,' said Faith. 'I have to have somebody to talk to, otherwise I begin to imagine bits of fat floating about just under the surface of the water.'

'Do you remember when we used to be able to buy rubber gloves for washing-up?' I said.

'Ha-ha!' said the Conductor. 'Those were the days!'

After that Charles and the Conductor told each other boiler stories, Faith telephoned home to find out if Little No-well was asleep and then it was time to wash-up. I washed, Faith dried, and the Conductor helped Charles to put things away. It was done in no time, but just as we were settling down in front of the fire the telephone rang, and Charles had to go out. As he had to go past their very door, it seemed silly that they shouldn't go with him, so they said good-bye and what a lovely evening it had been.

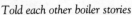

Told each other boiler stories

I sat in front of the fire for a bit, and turned on the news, and slept through it, and then I went to bed.

Charles came in about midnight. 'Was it a boy or a girl?' I said.

'Boy,' said Charles. 'Nothing but boys nowadays. I don't know what the world is coming to.'

'Little No-well will have a grand time when she grows up,' I said.

'Nice evening,' said Charles, clambering into bed. 'I always like having Faith and the Conductor—they're so interesting to talk to.'

Always your affectionate Childhood's Friend,

HENRIETTA

MY DEAR ROBERT
  I woke up suddenly last night and had the horrors. Horrors-in-the-Night, as everybody knows, are terrible. Remorse for all that you have done ill; regret (and this is even worse) for good that you have neglected to do; the ache of separation from those you love; and the silence of death—all these come crowding round you like goblins, and the knowledge that the whole thing is, according to Charles, due to wind in the lower bowel brings little comfort at two a.m., with the waves dragging across the shingle with a harsh and hopeless sound.

Since the war Horrors-in-the-Night have become well-nigh unbearable, and few people can remain in bed once an attack begins. Mrs Admiral once got up and made a cake during a bad bout, and I have more than once gone downstairs and played the piano until I felt better, but have had to give up this comfortable practice since our Evacuees came to live with us, for fear of disturbing the little boys, whose room is over the piano.

One of the nicest things about being married is that you have somebody to talk to if your Horrors-in-the-Night get completely out of hand, and though I always try to spare Charles, last night I found myself wallowing in such depths

that the only thing was
to lean out of bed and
touch his shoulder.

'What is the matter,
Henrietta?'

'Everything is so
awful, Charles.'

'Have a soda-mint,'
said Charles.

'I've had one.'

'Have you got War-
Horrors or just ordinary
Horrors-in-the-Night?'

'Both.'

'Poor Henrietta!'
said Charles.

'All this suffering,'
I said, 'and nothing but

*Mrs Admiral once got up
and made a cake*

greed and violence to build on when the war is over.'

'Have another soda-mint,' said Charles.

I had one. Then I said, 'Why are we here? That's
what I don't understand. Why be here at all when it all has
to be so beastly?'

'I suppose we just came, like mould on cheese.'

'Then why do we want to be happy? Mould on cheese
doesn't want to be happy.'

'We've developed that way. In a few million years,
mould on cheese may have all sorts of ideas.'

'It's an interesting thought, Charles.'

'And as for animals, they'll probably have moral
aspirations.'

'You mean that in a few million years dogs may be
handing round the bag in church?'

'Well—yes.'

There was silence for a few minutes while I digested

this unique idea. Then I said: 'Perry would look rather sweet, wouldn't he?'

'You take everything so literally, Henrietta,' said Charles.

'I can just see him in a black coat and stripy trousers—'

'And brown gloves and brown boots to match his tan markings——'

Charles laughed and I laughed, and the soda-mint flew out of my mouth. I had to light my torch to look for it and found it, almost at once, sticking to the eiderdown.

Then Charles said, 'For God's sake, let's get some sleep,' and in two minutes he was snoring gently. But I lay awake for a long time thinking of the human race growing like mould on cheese. It all seemed rather senseless and depressing, and it was a long time before I got to sleep.

The next day I went to see Lady B, who is in bed with bronchitis. She was sitting up, knitting socks for the sailors, and though I couldn't exactly say she was thin, there was a frail, transparent look about her which frightened me.

'How are you?' I said, and Fay peeped out from under the eiderdown and growled at me.

'As well as any old lady of seventy-eight with bronchitis has a right to be,' said Lady B cheerfully. 'Be quiet, Fay; it's only Henrietta.'

'You're trying your hardest to get better, aren't you?' I said, the memory of my Horrors-in-the-Night still clinging to me.

'Of course. Don't be silly, Henrietta. It would be very churlish not to try, when darling Charles is taking so much trouble over me.'

'But you wouldn't mind if you didn't get better?'

'Not a bit,' said Lady B, and began to count her stitches. When she came to the end of the line, she said: 'You mind too much about people dying.'

'I mind about you dying,' I said, and sat down on the end of the bed. Fay growled again. 'Charles said in the night that we just *came*, like mould on cheese, and it all seems pretty silly.'

'Mould my foot!' said Lady B briskly. 'We are the children of God. Doctors and scientists often have those quaint ideas but even they don't really believe them, though of course they feel they ought to, poor dears. Now, pass me my knitting, Henrietta dear, and let's talk about something that *really* matters.'

'Charles also said that in a few million years dogs might be handing round the bag in church.'

'What enthralling conversations you and Charles do have in the night!'

'We thought Perry would look rather sweet. So would Fay, of course,' I added hastily.

'Fay couldn't hand round the bag,' said Lady B firmly, 'she's a girl.'

Always your affectionate Childhood's Friend,

HENRIETTA

February 7, 1945

MY DEAR ROBERT
It was the Conductor's birthday last week, and he and Faith gave a lovely party. When we all got invitations on pre-war At Home cards with 'Games' in the right-hand corner, there was a good deal of talk and excitement.

'Games? What games?' said Colonel Simpkins, joining a little group outside the grocer's.

'I suppose they don't mean bridge,' said Mrs Savernack rather wistfully.

'Of course they don't mean bridge,' said Mrs Whinebite. 'They've asked Henrietta.'

Just then we saw Faith coming down the Street, pushing Little No-well in her pram. Little No-well was wearing a pink bonnet with nose and cheeks to match, and looked adorable.

'Hi, Faith!' shouted the Admiral. 'What are these Games at your party?'

Faith came quite close to us, opened her blue eyes very wide, and said, 'Kissing Games,' in a low, mysterious voice, and then wheeled Little No-well rapidly away down the Street.

'God bless my soul!' said Colonel Simpkins.

'But I don't *like* kissing,' said Mr Savernack, looking quite ill. 'If anybody kisses me, I shall be extremely annoyed.'

'I don't suppose anybody will,' said Mrs Savernack. 'Don't get in a State, Bernard.'

I could hardly bear to wait for the party, partly because I hadn't been to one for so long, and partly because I was so longing to wear an evening dress again. I decided on the red one which you used to like, Robert, and which hasn't had an outing since you and I danced at the Savoy just before the war; the time you stole a white carnation out of one of the vases for your buttonhole and I was cross with you. Do you remember?

Well, the day of the party came, and I was so determined not to be hurried over dressing that I started having a bath directly after tea. I put some of my most alluring bath-salts into it, and took a long time over my face and hair, and finished up with a little dab of scent behind the ears. I felt positively pre-war until I put on my only pair of evening stockings and found a ladder an inch wide reaching from ankle to knee. Breathing a prayer that none of the Games, kissing or otherwise, would expose the legs, I hurried downstairs.

'My word,' said Charles, 'you have got yourself up like a ham-bone!'

I could hardly take my eyes off Charles, whom I had not seen in a dinner jacket for years. He said he hoped that he wouldn't be called upon to stand on his head, as the moths had eaten a neat round hole in the seat of his trousers.

Unfortunately, the day of the party coincided with Evensong's night out, and by the time I had pinned up my skirt, dished up the dinner and washed up afterwards, my hair had come adrift, my eyeshadow had disappeared and my hands smelt of cabbage. However, there was no time to repair these ravages, as it was time for us to call for Lady B, who hurried out to the car with a shawl over her face.

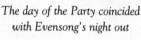

'Of course, you're mad to come out,' said Charles crossly.

'Nonsense, Charles!' said Lady B, who was attending

The day of the Party coincided with Evensong's night out

the party against her doctor's orders. 'It's done me good already. I'd forgotten how nice I looked in black velvet.'

'Before the evening's out,' I said in a very determined voice from the back of the car, 'I am going to kiss Mr Savernack.'

'Why Mr Savernack?' said Lady B.

'Because he hates it.'

'Then why kiss him, poor brute?' said Charles.

'I want to see what happens. He might find he liked it, after all, and sort of come to life.'

'Like the Sleeping Beauty,' said Lady B.

The party, when we got to it, was lovely. The house

was warm, and everybody was so pleased to see everybody else in different clothes that they went round congratulating each other on each other's appearance. Mr Savernack, with a determined, non-kissing expression on his face, went and wedged himself into a corner, thereby missing a lot of fun, because the Kissing Game didn't come on for a long time.

The Kissing Game was simple and very enjoyable. Somebody was blindfolded and stood in the middle of the room and pointed and said, 'Abe, are you there?' If it was a man, he said, 'Rebecca, are you there?' and then Abe (or Rebecca) got sheepishly from his or her chair and played Blind Man's Buff singles until caught, and kissed, to the joy of the beholders. When it came to my turn, I was blindfolded and turned round twice, but I felt the fire at my back, and knew that the cowering Mr Savernack must be on my right, so I pointed firmly in his direction and said firmly, 'Abe, are you there?'

There was a scuffling noise and no answer, so I took the bandage off my eyes and found Mr Savernack had deceitfully crept from his corner and was sitting between Charles and Lady B with a hunted expression on his face.

'You mustn't cheat, Henrietta,' said the Conductor, and he tied me up and twiddled me again, but this time so far from the fire that I didn't know where I was; but Lady B and Charles coughed in an obliging way, so I soon got my bearings and crept over to where I knew my victim must be.

'Abe, are you there?' I said, pointing an accusing finger.

There was a strangled cry and the door slammed, and Mrs Savernack said, 'I don't think he's feeling very well.'

As I couldn't very well pursue Mr Savernack into the hall, I went on with the game and eventually collared Colonel Simpkins, who behaved in a most gallant manner and said he couldn't think why we hadn't started kissing each other years ago.

After that we had a delicious supper, and then it was time to go home. As I was going upstairs to put on my coat, I saw Mr Savernack standing in the hall, bang under the mistletoe left over from Christmas. I leant over the banisters and kissed his brow.

Mr Savernack shuddered and turned green, not in the least like the Sleeping Beauty, and Mrs Savernack, coming out of the dining-room, said: 'I really cannot think, Henrietta, why you are making this dead set at Bernard. He's not That Sort of Man at all.'

I said, 'I know.'

Always your affectionate Childhood's Friend,

HENRIETTA

February 21, 1945

MY DEAR ROBERT
It was so warm a few days ago that I took Lady B to sit in the sun on the cliff path. It was hard to believe, as we sat there basking, that only a few days ago we had been slithering and slipping about on icy roads, with our feet tied up in dusters.

'This is very good for my bronchials,' said Lady B, closing her eyes and taking a few deep, rattling breaths.

'One could enjoy it more if one didn't keep thinking of the Russians,' I said.

Lady B opened her eyes and looked at me severely. 'I don't know what's come over you, Henrietta,' she said. 'There was a time when you used to enjoy simple pleasures, but now you're always worrying because you aren't being bombed, or fighting on the Western Front, or starving in an occupied country, or being tortured by the Gestapo. Instead of thanking the Good God that none of these things is happening to you and enjoying His beautiful sunshine, you keep whipping yourself with knotted cords, like a morbid old monk. It makes me quite cross.'

'Yes,' I said meekly.

'I'm as sorry about the thaw for the Russians as you are, but you and me moaning and groaning on the cliff path isn't going to make it any colder in East Prussia.'

'No,' I said.

'And here comes Rosemary with her new baby,' said Lady B.

Rosemary, one of the many pretty young mothers who gladden our eyes in this place, wheeled her pram up to our seat and sat down. Inside the pram was a very new, pink baby. A little boy of four, looking dashing in a beret, was holding on at the side.

'Of course, she's adorable,' said Lady B, after inspecting the baby.

'And so good,' said Rosemary. 'I wish Peter could see her.'

I looked at Rosemary. There were shadows under her eyes and lines on her face that used not to be there. 'You must get tired,' I said.

'Sometimes,' said Rosemary. 'Jeremy is a handful these days.'

'Not a handful,' said Jeremy with truculence.

'Yes, you are,' said his mother calmly. 'We have some battles, I can tell you,' she said turning to Lady B and me, 'but I win in the end.'

'Mummy wins in the end!' said Jeremy, shrieking with laughter.

'It's all very well for you to laugh, you Imp,' said Lady B, 'but you're wearing your mother out.'

'Of course, I think children of between two and four are frightful,' I said.

'I couldn't agree with you more,' said Rosemary.

'And then, between five and six they suddenly get sweet again.'

'I'm glad to hear it,' said Rosemary, standing up. 'Come along, Jeremy; we must go home,' and she kissed her hand to us and wheeled the pram away.

'There goes a good girl,' said Lady B.

'All the young mothers ought to have George Medals,' I said. 'Toiling away year after year, never off the chain, and always torn with anxiety about their husbands.'

'I wish we could do something for them,' said Lady B.

'At one time I wanted to start a Young Mothers' Club, where they could drop in of an afternoon with their prams and dump the children in a communal nursery and have tea in peace.'

'Who was going to look after the children?'

'Not me. But, anyhow, Charles said they'd all give each other measles and whooping-cough, so I abandoned the idea.'

'All the same, I don't see why we shouldn't give them an evening party when the children are in bed,' said Lady B, sitting up very straight and with a gleam in her eye.

'Who would look after the children?'

'Grandfathers,' said Lady B firmly. 'Grandfathers and others.'

When Lady B makes up her mind to something it generally comes off, and so did this—in our house. Finding guardians for the children wasn't as difficult as I thought it would be. The Grandfathers came forward in a most gallant way, supplemented by Grandmothers and Others. Even the Admiral, who wasn't a grandfather, and now, alas! would never be one, volunteered to take on Jeremy the Handful and his baby sister. Faith had three mothers and their babies to spend the night in her house, because the Conductor is so absolutely reliable, and little Mrs Simpkins went with Colonel Simpkins because he was nervous of being left alone with twin girls of two.

Although we told them it was not in any way a grand party, the Young Mothers chose to come in long frocks. They said it was more of a treat that way. Charles insisted upon being present, although he was the only man. He said that as he had brought most of the babies into the world, he'd like to know who had a better right to be there than he. We had candles on the table and dessert, and what Charles calls Port of a Sort.

Several Grandfathers rang up during dinner to say the children were sleeping peacefully, and once Rosemary had a long, earnest conversation with the Admiral, in which we heard her say: 'And be *very* careful with the safety-pin.'

Later the Admiral rang up to say the baby was now asleep and Jeremy had decided to go into the Navy.

At the end of dinner, when our glasses were filled, Charles stood up. 'Ladies,' he said, 'I wish to propose a toast, though only three of us here can drink it. "To the Unsung Heroines of the War—God bless their pretty faces." '

'To the Unsung Heroines of the War'

Lady B and I stood up and said 'Hear, hear,' and took large gulps of the Port of a Sort, which tasted like sherry and cider mixed, and the Young Mothers opened their eyes very wide and said: 'What, *us*?'

Afterwards, in the drawing-room, they sat about, most of them on the floor, and talked about leave, and the homes they were going to have when the war was over. I saw a tear trickle down Lady B's cheek, and Rosemary said: 'Why, Lady B! You're crying!'

Lady B said, 'Don't take any notice of me. I've been having bronchitis.'

Then it was time for ten o'clock feeds and 'holdings out,' so they put on their thick shoes in the hall, tied handkerchiefs over their heads, kissed Lady B and Charles and me, and trudged off into the night.

Always your affectionate Childhood's Friend,

HENRIETTA

My Dear Robert   April 4, 1945
'Hatred,' said Lady B, laying down the paper, 'is a very silly thing.'

'Who's hating who?' said Faith.

Lady B put on her spectacles again and picked up the paper. 'The Middle West of America seems to be hating us,' she said.

'How odd,' said Faith; 'we don't hate them.'

'We shall soon if they go on like this,' said the Conductor, who was weeding the path close by.

'Oh, no,' said Lady B. 'That wouldn't get us anywhere. Besides, there's no excuse for us to hate the Middle West. Nobody's working on us as they are on them.'

'Who's working on them?' said Faith.

'Germans,' said the Conductor, pulling up an enormous bit of groundsel with an air of triumph.

'Little No-well, you are *not* to eat leaves,' said Faith, and she got up and picked her baby out of a flower-bed. Little No-well was wearing a pale pink cardigan, and her eyes were the colour of those expensive, large, deep-blue forget-me-nots.

'Little No-well, how sweet you are,' I said, as I always do when I look at her.

'I wish you wouldn't, Henrietta,' said Faith for the hundredth time. 'She's beginning to Understand.'

Lady B was still reading the paper. 'There seem to be some people called Blue Star Mothers who are behaving in a very peculiar manner,' she said.★

'Blue Star Mothers?' said Faith. 'How sweet!'

'Pah!' said the Conductor.

'What are they doing, anyway?' I said.

Lady B put down the paper and looked distressed. 'They seem to think we started the war, and are going to gorge ourselves with food, when everybody else is starving.'

'Monstrous!' said Faith pink with anger.

'Germans,' said the Conductor, and walked away to the rubbish heap with his basket.

'And yet,' said Lady B, 'the funny thing is that if some Blue Star Mothers were sitting here with us now, they'd be saying how sweet Little No-well is, and asking if she'd had trouble with her teeth.'

'If they said Little No-well was sweet I should like them,' said Faith, in a burst of honesty.

★In America, families would display a blue star in the window for each member of the household in the military and a gold star for those who had died. Understandably, these Blue Star Mothers—or the organisations that developed—tended to be very patriotic, somewhat isolationist and deeply suspicious of anything that might lead to the sending of more of 'our boys to die in foreign wars'.

'Of course you would,' said Lady B, 'and they'd like us. We'd all be friends.'

' "Buddies" is the word,' I said.

'It's all very distressing,' said Faith. 'I wish you hadn't told me, Lady B. I never read the paper. I just look after the Conductor and Little No-well and think about the new baby in August. I don't like thinking about Blue Star Mothers.'

'Nobody does,' said Lady B. 'But we must.'

'I shall have an ugly baby if I do,' said Faith.

'Nonsense!' said Lady B.

'I know!' said Faith. 'Let's start a Society of Pink Star Mothers and tour America and be frightfully friendly.'

'If you think I'm going to drag my family across the world in a spirit of good-will towards Blue Star Mothers,' said the Conductor, who had returned from the rubbish heap, 'you are making a big mistake. Home is the place for little children,' he said, and he picked Little No-well tenderly out of another flower-bed and took a leaf out of her mouth.

'What do you think we ought to do about it, Lady B?' I said, for Lady B is kind and wise and has sensible answers to most things.

Lady B wrinkled her forehead. '*I* don't know,' she said. 'I suppose if we keep open minds, and read both sides, and don't fly off the handle, it will help. When I remember all my dear, my very dear American friends, I find it very hard to believe that what this paper says is true.'

'Goodness knows I've been friendly to the Americans,' said Faith.

'I'll say you have,' said the Conductor, with some bitterness.

'Nothing will ever destroy those friendships,' said Lady B, '*nothing*,' but she sighed as she said it.

Just then we heard Faith's garden gate click. 'It's the Wash!' said Faith rapturously.

174

The lawn where we were sitting was round the corner, so we couldn't see what was coming up the garden path, but we could hear it. Shuffle, click, scrape—shuffle, click, scrape.

'What the hell——' said the Conductor.

'Not the Wash,' said Faith sadly.

'It sounds like a wild animal to me,' said Lady B, and Faith picked Little No-well up in her arms.

Shuffle, click, scrape. And then round the corner came George—our George—our American. One of his legs was in plaster, and he was dragging himself along on crutches. His smiling face, once so round and pink, was thin and drawn, but there he was—George, our George, giving the lie to the Blue Star Mothers.

'George!' we said.

'Well, it's certainly fine to see you folks again,' said George.

Then we all rushed at him. Lady B and Faith and I all kissed him, and the Conductor, his face white with emotion, wrung his hand.

George looked rather surprised. 'What a welcome!' he said, as we led him to the seat. 'Why, Henrietta, you're crying! And Lady B, too.' He took out his handkerchief and wiped our wet cheeks.

We led him to the seat

'Don't look at me like that, Faith, Honey. I'm not a ghost.'

'Oh, George,' said Lady B, 'you don't know how glad we are to see you.'

175

'You do like us, don't you, George?' I said earnestly.

'But you're my friends,' said George simply. 'Here, what is all this, anyway? Have I gone crazy or have you?'

'It's the Blue Star Mothers,' said Faith.

'Aw, *them*!' said George with contempt.

Always your affectionate Childhood's Friend,

HENRIETTA

May 16, 1945

M^Y DEAR ROBERT
'I am dreaming of a white August,' I sang, as I made a dash for the greenhouse. Lady B followed me, panting and brushing the snow from her coat. There we found the Conductor lovingly pressing little tomato plants into pots.

'Conductor!' I gasped, quite overwhelmed by this generosity.

'They're a Peace Present from Faith and Little No-well and me,' said the Conductor.

Just then Faith and Little No-well arrived at the greenhouse door. Little No-well had a tiny snowflake melting on her nose and seemed to think it very funny. I kissed them both and the Conductor as well, and thanked them for my lovely Peace Present, and the Conductor said he hoped the Germans would give in before the plants grew up and we ate all the tomatoes. Then we sat down on upturned flower-pots, while the snow fell gently, with a whispering sound, on the glass over our heads.

'What are you going to do on VE Day, Henrietta?' said Lady B.

'Stop weeding,' I said.

'If you stop for long the bindweed will get the better of you,' said the Conductor.

'I didn't say I was going to stop weeding for ever: I said I was going to stop for VE Day. I shall lie down on my bed with a hot-water bottle and a trashy novel. What are you going to do, Lady B?'

'Go to church,' said Lady B. 'And then I shall come up here and interrupt Henrietta's reading. You know, I don't think it's really safe for me to sit on this flower-pot,' and she got up and perched on the shelf with the tomato plants.

'If it's anything like a day, we're going to take Little No-well for a picnic to the bluebell wood,' said Faith. 'And while we're there we're going to choose a name for the New-Baby-in-August.'

'That will be a lovely thing to do,' said Lady B.

'And when he's old enough to ask questions——'

'Or she,' said the Conductor, who secretly yearns for another daughter.

'——and says "Why did you call me——?" (whatever it is we do call him), we shall say, "We thought of it in the bluebell wood on VE Day." '

'And he'll say to himself, "How they do go on about that old VE Day, poor dears." '

'I hope so,' said the Conductor. 'One of the things I love about Little No-well is that she doesn't know anything about the war,' and he put his hand tenderly on his baby's golden head.

'They'll know about it all right,' said Lady B. 'I don't suppose the mess will be cleared up by the time they start asking questions.'

'If it ever is cleared up,' said Faith gloomily.

'Sometimes,' I said, 'I feel absolutely hopeless about the future. *Hopeless!*'

Just then there was a loud cracking sound and Lady B

and the tomato plants slid down the shelf on which they were sitting and landed with a crash in the corner. 'Darling Lady B, are you hurt?' we all cried, and rushed to pick her up. Little No-well set up a wail.

Lady B and the tomato plants slid down

'I don't think so,' said Lady B, feeling her arms and legs. 'No, I'm not. Dear me, bone-meal in the hair! How very unpleasant. Just take that bit of bass off my hat, will you, somebody? Little No-well, darling, I can't bear it if you cry, and oh, my goodness, look at the tomato plants!'

They were indeed a sorry sight. Broken flower-pots and earth in a heap in the corner, and here and there a pathetic green leaf poking through.

'Hopeless!' I said.

'Henrietta,' said Lady B tartly, 'that is twice in two minutes you've said "Hopeless!" You'd better ask Charles for a tonic.'

'Yes, Lady B,' I said meekly.

'Now, come along,' said Lady B, 'and let's get this all tidied up.'

We set to work and began delving tentatively in the

wreckage for the tomato plants. Only two were broken, and soon the others were planted firmly in new pots and the debris heaped in a basket. Little No-well stopped crying and smeared herself with wet mud in a corner.

'There!' said Lady B, straightening her back. 'You see, it wasn't so hopeless after all. Nothing ever is if you set to work with a will. And that, Henrietta darling, is my Great Thought for the day. And now I must go home and wash the bone-meal out of my hair.'

Then the snow stopped and the sun came out, and suddenly the greenhouse became as hot as a greenhouse, and we all rushed panting out into the fresh air.

Always your affectionate Childhood's Friend,

HENRIETTA

May 30, 1945

MY DEAR ROBERT
Well! So we've beaten the Germans at last, and I don't suppose I shall have to write you many more letters. All the same, writing to you has become such a habit I shall probably go on penning you long, chatty letters and dropping them over our garden wall onto your asparagus-bed. Which reminds me that I am sorry to have to tell you that bindweed has reared its ugly head among your asparagus. I pointed this out to your tenants, but I won't tell you what they said in reply—decency forbids.

Charles and I started VE Day in sober mood. 'After all,' we said to each other, 'we haven't beaten the Japs yet, and we haven't suffered like London has.' We didn't even crack open the bottle of champagne which we have been talking about for the last five years, but decided to keep it for when Bill and the Linnet's Philip come home. I went to church, and Charles rushed out of the house muttering something about Major Operations. It was Evensong's day off, so I didn't even lie down with my hot-water bottle and the trashy novel I had promised myself, but bumbled about the house feeling unaccountably tired.

We asked the Admiral and Mrs Admiral to come and share our evening stew, and they arrived with their own beef and carrots in a little bowl to add to our casserole, because, they said, it would make them unhappy to think they were eating our rations.

'I'm afraid this is a rather sad day for you,' said Charles, giving Mrs Admiral a hug.

'No, Charles,' said Mrs Admiral, 'though of course, we are thinking of our dear boys.'

'I think they both enjoyed their lives,' said the Admiral, 'and they certainly gave us a great deal of happiness.' Then he cleared his throat and said, 'This is a very good cocktail, Charles. What have you put in it?'

'A little Vodka,' said Charles, 'in honour of our gallant Allies.'

'Vodka, eh?' said the Admiral, smacking his lips. 'I'm beginning to understand why the Russian parties go on until six o'clock in the morning.'

We soon began to feel quite gay, and by the time we had finished the washing-up we were longing to celebrate, but the village was as quiet as it had been every night, except for air raids, ever since the beginning of the war.

'If only the black-out had been lifted,' said Mrs Admiral with a sigh, 'they might have thought of something to do.'

'Listen!' said Charles. We all listened and heard the sound of music and singing. The next minute Evensong came panting up the garden path. 'There's a Caper going on down the Street,' she said, 'and they're asking for Doctor Charles.'

'Come on!' shouted Charles, and he tore down to the gate.

In the Street, where I have spent so many unhappy shopping hours, a 'Praaper ole Caper,' as we say, was indeed in progress, and conveniently adjacent to the pub. Some large-hearted Resident had allowed his piano to be dragged out onto the pavement, and before I knew where I was I was seated before it playing 'Annie Laurie' on as many notes as still felt like sounding. As you know, Robert, I am but a poor performer on the piano at the best of times, and now, with everybody crowding round me, pressing my elbows into my side, with soldiers breathing beer on me, and children shrilling into my ears until my head buzzed like an alarm-clock, I felt I was giving a poor performance. But nobody seemed to mind. Everybody was yelling, and on the outskirts of the crowd a group of independent-minded Marines were singing different songs all together. Charles put half a pint of beer on the piano, and between 'Loch Lomond' and 'The Old Folks at Home' I took a grateful swill, but next time I looked for it, it had gone.

After a time a Marine appeared who said he could play dance music, and I gladly gave up my place at the piano to him, for my fingers were giving out, and so was my repertoire. The Marine began playing 'When I Grow Too Old to Dream' with his right hand and something quite different with his left. This absence of harmony, so prevalent among the piano-playing youth of today, always worries me, but I know that Rhythm Is All, and I try not to mind.

Charles was by now revolving in a very stately manner with a lady in a red hat; Lady B, equally stately, was in the arms of Mr Pook, from the bacon counter, and the Admiral was making many impressive swoops and twirls with a Land Army girl, who laughed so much that she fell down twice.

Faith, prevented from dancing because of the New-Baby-in-August, plucked at my sleeve. 'Dance with our Canadian,' she said.

'Can't we find a girl for him?' I said.

'No,' said Faith. 'He's just out of a prison camp, and sometimes he feels bad and can't talk. He wouldn't mind with you.'

The Canadian's arm, when he put it round me, was tense. So was his face. 'You dance very beautifully,' I said.

'Do I? I haven't had any practice—for a long time.'

'I know. This is how the English enjoy simple pleasures.'

'It's fine,' said the Canadian.

'Everybody is very glad to have you here, you know.'

'I like to be here,' said the Canadian. Then he saw the Land Army girl and the Admiral fall down for the second time, and he gave a sudden snort of laughter.

Laughed so much she fell down twice

Then people began shouting 'Bonfire!' and there, at the other end of the Street, was the beginning of a very healthy one. The Marines were throwing their love letters onto the flames in an abandoned manner which I felt would not have been appreciated by their writers, and people came rushing out of the houses with bundles of what would undoubtedly have been salvage if they hadn't lost their heads. We made a huge ring and danced around as other people were doing all over England, but soon it was black-

182

out time and the police arrived to say that there really might be submarines in the bay. They threw water on the bonfire and put it out, but you could see they hated doing it.

Then we took Lady B home, because Charles was afraid the Caper might be too much for her heart, though she said she didn't mind if it was.

When last I saw the Canadian he had a pretty girl on each side of him and was singing 'Auld lang Syne'.

Always your affectionate Childhood's Friend,

HENRIETTA